D0805843

The Agony of Fashion

The Agony of Fashion

Eline Canter Cremers-van der Does

English translation
Leo Van Witsen

BLANDFORD PRESS
Poole *Dorset*

First published in the U.K. 1980

First published as *Onze Lijne Door De Tijd* by Moussault's Uitgeverij B.V., Baarn, Netherlands

British Library Cataloguing in Publication Data

Canter Cremers-Van der Does, Eline
The agony of fashion.
1. Costume – History
I. Title
391'.009 GT511

ISBN 0 7137 1058 6

Photoset in 10/12pt V.I.P. Palatino and set, printed and bound by Fakenham Press Limited, Fakenham, Norfolk.

Contents

Colour Plates

Introduction

Mankind (woman in particular) has through the ages reshaped the body in order to be beautiful and to obtain the figure, the silhouette or 'line' which the current fashion decrees.

Is it possible to reshape the body at will? Yes, it can be done: add a little here, pare down a little there and we feel like a different person.

'Paring down' is accomplished through pain and tears, but we are glad to make the sacrifice in order to be beautiful. 'Adding on' is achieved through ingenious padding and the use of mysterious appliances. This book hopes to lift a tip of the veil that shrouds these beauty secrets.

Deformations are not exclusively the demand of an ideal beauty through centuries of our civilization and super-civilization. Primitive man, who, because of climatic conditions, or lack of raw materials, hardly wore any clothes at all, painted and tattooed himself with great care, kneaded the malleable heads of newborn children to a point, and stretched necks, genitals and lower lips.

We speak with horror of mutilation of the Chinese girl's feet, as it was done in the past, but forget the compressed

1. Deformation:
1. Apparatus for the shaping of a pointed head (Central America).
2. African woman with a 'platter-lip'.
3. Feet of a Chinese woman.
4. Papua girl with decorative relief-tattooing.
5. Earlobe in Nias.

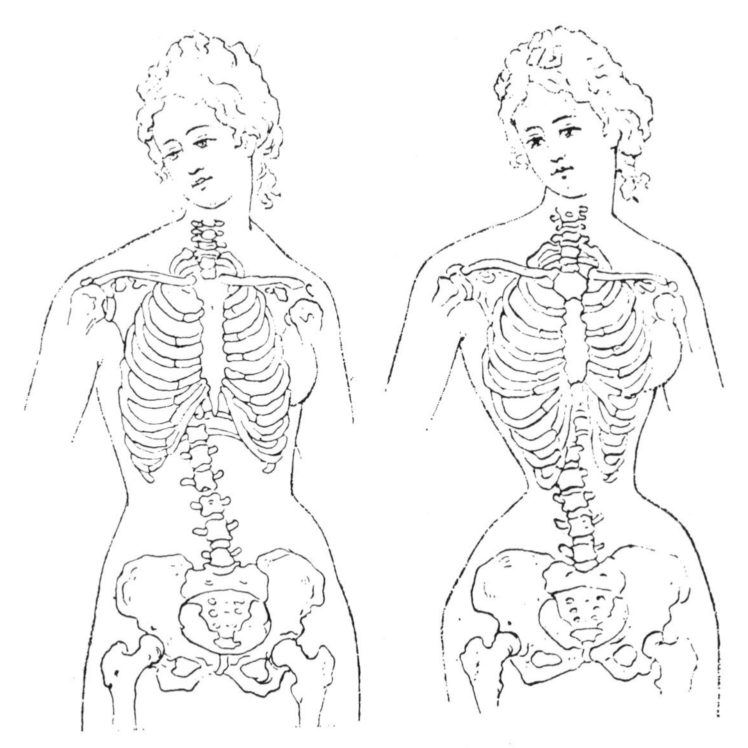

2. Normal ribs (left) and the ribs of our great-grandmothers (right), according to Dr C. H. Stratz.

ribcages of our tightly corseted grandmothers. After all, binding the feet clearly had a social and psychological purpose: to maintain the distinction between a lady of the leisure classes and the large-footed working slave. Bound feet were delicate and small, arousing protective feelings in the opposite sex, while the retarded blood circulation in the lower extremities, which were the result of this custom, caused a heightened blood propulsion in other parts of the body.

Does this 'paring down' and 'adding on' exist for men as well? Yes it does, although to a lesser degree. 'Paring down' is not hard for a woman: the fatty tissue in many parts of her body is readily displaced and can through the use of corsets be pushed upward or downward. The bust, which consists partly of fatty tissue, has through the ages been compressed, enlarged, pushed up or down between neck and waist at the whim of the fashion barometer.

The bones and muscles of men are less suited to such

reshaping. Only in the eighteenth century did the man lace his waist in a corset. It improved the fit of his small-waisted, full-skirted coat. In the next century the horse riding military man gave himself a proud posture and a small waist through the use of tight corseting. But as for 'adding on' men have reached for this means of appearing beautiful (strong and masculine) just as much as women have.

When you walk behind a well-dressed man, in a suit and an overcoat, observe the robustly arched chest and back, how handsomely wide he is from shoulder to elbow, only to dwindle from thereon down to a skinny little fellow. Around 1955 this excessive padding eased a little, but time and again, from the fifteenth century onward, the artificial broadening of the shoulders can be observed in male fashions.

This shape of the body, this silhouette, produced by our clothes, determines our image of a period and of a fashion.

1 Egypt

The Egyptians were slender and emphasized this 'line' by their mode of dressing: hip cloths, skirts and shawls were pulled tightly around the body and many plaited clothes produced a knitted effect. This slender silhouette seemed slimmer still in contrast with the woman's very broad and large wigs and the men's widely extending, heavily starched

3. Relief showing slender Egyptian women.

headcloths. (In the same manner our grandmothers, pre-1914, made their tight hobble skirt seem tighter still by wearing enormously wide-brimmed hats.)

About 500 B.C., during the reign of Queen Hatseput (sister and wife of Tutmosis II), three ships sailed through the Red Sea to Punt, 'the land of incense'. (Whether that was present-day Eritrea, Somalia and Kenya we do not know, although the arrival and departure of this voyage are depicted in reliefs in the Egyptian mausoleum temples at Der-el-Bahri.) The departure must have pleased the Egyptians of that time: a rich booty of baskets, sacks, vats with provisions, and incense trees in pots were carefully loaded on board by the crew. There were even baboons in the boat, seated on a rope stretched across especially for that purpose. However, the representation of the arrival must have caused a sensation. Not only was the Egyptian envoy greeted by the King of Punt with offerings of precious gifts—golden rings, elephant tusks—but the Queen who approached with a smile to greet him was probably fatter than any woman an Egyptian had ever seen. The relief carver evidently rejoiced in adding flabby wads of fat to her already voluminous arms and legs.

4. The king of Punt with spouse and suite welcomes the Egyptian Ambassador. Relief from Der-el-Bahri.

2 The Pre-Christian East

Assyria, Babylonia, Persia, the biblical lands

One hears little about the body's 'line' in connection with the old cultures of the eastern Mediterranean. Carved images do exist of men in fringed woollen cloths (Assyria, Babylonia), in leather hauberks or silken garments (Persia), but there is no sign of underclothing, which is important in creating different silhouettes. Crete is an exception in this respect, a small waist was strived for: the man girdled himself with a tight belt, the woman made her waist small and supported her breasts with a smooth leather bodice. (These may be considered the forerunners of all corset bodices, which were to be replaced by brassières towards 1900.)

Little is known of the clothes of eastern women. In the South and East they did not leave the house, being strictly confined in women's quarters, harems and purdas, and were not depicted in carvings or murals.

The little evidence that has been preserved consists of two small reliefs. One shows an Assyrian Queen, the other portrays a Babylonian lady. Both are wrapped in large woollen shawls; behind them are a male and a female slave, who waft cool breezes with a fan. Each lady has a tall and intricate coiffure. A great deal of what has survived is connected with the care of the skin and hair: combs, mirrors, make-up containers, perfume bottles, and sticks to apply eye-liners. More was done than merely lending nature a helping hand.

Neither the shape of the Assyrian King's beard nor the coiffure of his servant are natural in the least. Many hours of tonsorial artistry and many bottles of fixature and brilliantine must have been used to line up all those curls in such even rows. To obtain skin oil, Egyptian pyramid builders would go on strike; in the Bible more can be read about ointments than about clothes.

5. 1, 2. *Assyrian king and servant hunting, c.850 B.C.*
3. *Cretan woman with pushed-up bust. Fresco from Knosos, 1450–1400 B.C. in the Heraklion museum.*

The *fasciae* (bindings), about which more will be heard in chapter 3, were probably used in biblical lands; also Isaiah (3:16–24) warns 'the daughters of Zion' that as a punishment for their haughty behaviour their 'bindings' and 'garters' would be taken from them. (Translator's note: The King James version gives no equivalent words for these terms. Most likely what is being alluded to are the bands that were worn to support the breasts and those beautifully coloured braids which fastened to the sole of the sandals and wound around the legs.)

Except for Assyrian soldiers, who wore some kind of netting underneath their high open sandals, stockings were not worn in the Orient, and consequently no garters either in our sense of the word.

3 Greece

At the time of the reform movement (around 1900) when the relationship between clothes and health was at long last realized, the fight against the corset began. One of the arguments used in favour of its banishment was that in ancient Greece women had ideal figures and yet did not wear corsets. This was a completely incorrect assumption.

What is an *ideal figure*? We will demonstrate that this ideal swings widely between the stance of the fifteenth century with the heavy, pushed-out abdomen, and the flat, nay even hollow flanks of the *droit devant* and *plus que droit* around the turn of the present century. *Every fashion demands a different figure and the 'ideal' is only the very latest, at the moment that we are tired of looking at what just preceded it.* That applies to our figures as well as to our clothes.

This changing fashion-ideal affects many aspects of social life. For instance, ideas about what are ideal and fashionable *Social engagements* have changed. Our great-grandfathers would not have attended cocktail parties, nor would today's teenagers dream of going to a ball or a tea-party. In *sport* croquet is not the popular game it once was. Riding a bicycle was daring and fashionable in the 1880s and 1890s before the advent of the motor car. Now the bicycle is once again coming into fashion. Fashion affects our *choice of home* as the preference for houses or flats changes with different generations. It applies to our *health*: sometimes it is fashionable to be pale and fragile, seeking protection and at other times smart, sporting and robust. The fashion-ideal affects our entire life: man happens to be a very 'imitative' being who will follow every fashion, consciously or unconsciously.

In one respect Greek girls had the advantage over their sisters of the 'Reform Era' of the 1890s: they were raised on sports, the dance and gymnastics, which activities make much support from corsets unnecessary. The reform girls, by contrast, performed gymnastics only once a week (if they attended a progressive school, that is) and the sudden omission of the corset would have ill served her flaccid muscles.

In fact, Greek women *were* corseted. It started at birth. Infants were carefully swaddled—their arms were not permitted any motion until they were six months old. Plato even proposed that children should be constrained in that fashion up to and inclusive of the age of two. In addition each arm was wrapped individually from hand to shoulder and so was each leg; next the entire child was wrapped in swaddling clothes and was thus prevented from becoming cross-eyed through touching its eyes with its hands!

In the province of Lacedonia, however, infants were left to grow entirely unhampered. Unfortunately no medical statistics of that time are known to us to prove that a Lacedonian baby was healthier and straighter of body and limb than a child from the other provinces. Pictures from *The Mirror of Illustrious Women* (1606) by Theocritum a Ganda (Daniël Heinsius) might serve as proof however. They were shown in the exhibition 'The Woman in Prints' at the Museum Boymans Beuningen, Rotterdam in 1975/6. In the print 'The woman of Sparta' a tapestry worker proudly shows her product to a Spartan woman, who in return displays her (unswaddled) children as proof of her more important achievement. Vain mothers wound these woollen or linen wrappings (the *fascia*) around the torsos of their daughters for the purpose of keeping the girls straight and slender. If, after

6. 1. *A woman clamps one end of the* fascia *under her armpit in order to wrap it around her. Greek statuette in Florence.*
2. *The binding of the* fascia *above the breast.*
3. *A baby swaddled in* fasciae.

all that, they were still too fat, they were simply given less to eat. The adult woman bound the *fascia* under her breasts, directly on the bare skin; therefore *fascia pectoralis* (breast binder) was a forerunner of our 'bra'. This firm bust, pushed up high, gives a beautiful line to long garments that would otherwise fall limp and seem shapeless. Greek clothing was not cut and sewn: pliable rectangular woollen cloths were caught at the shoulder with a clasp and held in place by *one* or *two* girdles. A large, heavier piece of cloth was draped as a mantle, was used to cover the chilly marble seats, or as a blanket on the bed. Men wore the same draped cloths, but theirs were shorter.

7. Breast binders painted on Greek vases, c.400 B.C. Museum in Geneva.

In fig. 6 a woman clasps one end of the *fascia* under her armpit in order to be able to wrap it tightly. Women who considered their bust too large flattened it with the *fascia*, pulling it tightly across the breasts. (Fig. 7 shows that tapes were used. They never fail to be present when these wrappings appear in pictures on Greek vases.) A slave probably helped with the stretching of these wrappings and tapes. Fat Greek women were willing to sacrifice a great deal for the sake of beauty: in the summer it must have been hot and oppressive to be so tightly bound.

Just like bodices and *décolletages* in later centuries, the *fascia* were used to hide things such as a *billet doux*, money or a token of love.

4 Rome

The woman

The Roman woman's clothing worked on the Greek principle of draping or wrapping oneself in rectangular pieces of cloth. More layers of clothes were worn because the climate in Italy is colder than in Greece, and because less wool was worn in favour of linen and silk. Here also the bust was supported by wrappings, but these were worn in many colours for decorative purposes: transparent ones were used under thin fabric, or they might be worn bound around the legs. Otherwise no changes in the silhouette occurred. Beautiful imports from the colonies like embroideries from Babylon, thin silken fabrics from the Greek islands of Kos and Amorgos, dey-stuffs from Asia Minor, and the blonde tresses of Germanic women—all served to satisfy the Roman lady's vanity.

The man

Men also wrapped themselves in several layers of garments. The Roman burgher draped himself proudly in his enormous toga (three times the body length) which slaves were forbidden to wear.

Until far into the Middle Ages, the man of prominence cloaked himself in long garments, while the serf, the labourer or the soldier wore short clothes. Firstly, it is logical that at work, in battle or at the hunt, men did not want their movement hindered by long clothes, but, secondly, a person's dignity could be measured by the amount of room he or she occupied in space. Hence the voluminous togas for judges, the ample church vestments for prelates, the long trains, the coronation mantles, etc.

The Roman state gave the greatest consideration to its military dress, which was handsome, practical and offered protection against the stabs of spears and arrows, as well as sabre cuts. The Roman soldier used leg wrappings for the support of his calves on long marches, in the same way as puttees were used in the First World War.

Only one small change deserves mention, in the natural appearance of the man's body: the Southern and Oriental man disliked body-hair. The Koran prescribed its depilation, something that was accomplished more easily and less painfully when hair and skin were first softened by the heat and steam of the bath houses. In many Roman and Oriental baths there was consequently the constant din of masseurs and depilators clamouring for their customers. They would perhaps do this more loudly in order to drown out their victims' yells of pain, while the hairs were being pulled from their armpits.

In oriental countries men bathed first, women afterwards. This left the ladies with dirty water in which the men's extracted hairs were floating among the soap suds.

5 Roman Empire - The East

(after A.D. 395)

The Roman Empire declined, and in A.D. 395 moved eastward, with Byzantium, the present-day Istanbul, as its capital. Christianity became the state religion, which did not stem the political decline. Eventually these regions were conquered by Islam.

This was an important time in the realm of textiles: in imperial workshops the most sumptuous silken fabrics were woven and subsequently exported. Men's linen tunics were decorated with embroidery and with woven pieces of coloured wool.

Shoes, made of coloured leather, were of great refinement. Jewels, real, and already simulated, were worn in abundance. Amid so much finery, vanity and the craving for luxury were satisfied and no change in the body's 'line' was sought.

Many traces of the Byzantine culture are still to be found in the Balkan countries.

6 The Early Middle Ages

North-western Europe until 1200

The early Middle Ages were not exactly times to spend much thought on the body's 'line': life was raw, sober and harsh.

People knew how to spin and weave from earliest times and, with a pointed thorn used as a needle, very simple chemise-like garments were made. Women usually wore a skirt over the chemise, and men drawers under it. There was no hint of tailoring: everything was loose, tied around the waist with a cord or a girdle. Leather and animal skins were also worn. Pieces of cloth were sometimes fastened at the shoulder with a *fibula* (not unlike our safety pin), or the girdle was closed with a beautiful clasp. The art of forging metal was a very old one in the northern regions. In countries like Sweden and Russia examples can be found that are unequalled today despite the advantages of our modern tools.

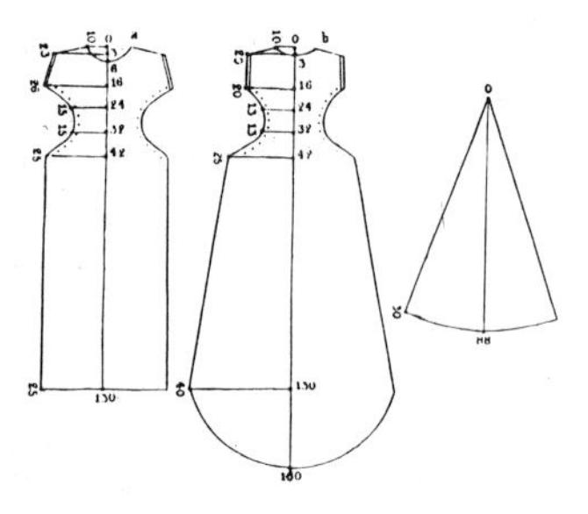

8. First attempt to make the waist small, the skirt full. Pattern from E. von Sichart. Twelfth century.

The Roman legions moved northward along the great rivers, and far into England. When centuries later they in turn were expelled by the savage tribes, during the great migration (fourth to sixth centuries), they left behind their buildings, ships, household wares, clothes, etc.

In A.D. 800 Charlemagne founded the Holy Roman

Empire, which comprised a large part of Europe. Christianity was by now generally accepted. The cloisters were centres for science and education, although it was unusual if the knight in his castle could read and write.

More attention was paid to clothing, but it remained straight and loose because closings were not known: everything had to be put on over the head. At best there would be a short slit at the neck, which was laced together with a string.

9. The devil of fashion. English manuscript. Twelfth century.

The woman

Around A.D. 1000 this small laced slit was developed in a different way. A pointed section was cut from the side seams of chemise or gown, and small holes on either side of the edge of the seams were laced together. This achieved what women had yearned for for centuries—a tiny waist! The corset was born: eroticism of dress was discovered! In order to call attention to other parts of the body it was sought to contrast them with the small waist, which appeared more brittle, more exquisite, and more desirable between voluminous sleeves and above the ample folds of long skirts and trains. It even seems that fox tails were sewn inside the chemise in order to give to hips and bosom a wanton roundness in contrast to the tightly laced waist. This feminine vanity was immediately disapproved of, and forbidden by the clergy, and probably encouraged just because of that. The forbidden fruit tastes ever sweet.

The use of a great amount of fabric to achieve fullness of skirts and sleeves was considered a superfluous luxury; and a display of the body was deemed sinful. There appeared in about 1200 a caricature in an English prayer book (fig. 9). The caricature seems to cry: 'For shame!' It is the first 'For shame!' in fashion history. 'Behold those lacings, how long the train, how ample the sleeve!'

The man

The man wore a linen shirt and loincloth, or short full drawers, gathered under a girdle. Later they were held around the waist by a drawstring. Around his legs, which were increasingly accentuated, he wore sewn stockings: hose, or leggings which were attached to the girdle with a leather thong (a sort of garter). A long or short tunic was worn over that.

Men of the early Middle Ages were not concerned with their body 'line' but noblemen and their courtiers liked to wear silk (although Charlemagne preferred the simple, rough Frisian wool). Later on the crusaders had to embark at the Italian silk centres of Venice and Genoa which encouraged the use of silk.

10. Woman with tightly laced gown. Chartres Cathedral. c.1150.

11. One of the wise virgins, without a laced waist, in the dome at Magdeburg. c.1200.

7 The Late Middle Ages

(1200–1500)

In the thirteenth century great changes occurred in the sphere of fashion:

1. From the East the crusaders brought many handsome objects in the realm of textiles such as embroideries and tapestries. These increasingly offered the opportunity to decorate and thereby change the look of clothes.
2. International encounters at crusades and tournaments increased the desire for beautiful clothes.
3. The guilds were founded; the making of clothes, which was a home industry before, now became a *craft*.
4. The *button-closing* was invented; clothes no longer had to be pulled on over the head, but could be buttoned tightly in front for a slim look.

It is precisely the combination of the last two factors that created a 'tailor' out of the erstwhile clothes-maker; made to measure patterns had arrived.

The woman with her tight lacings already had a dress that clearly accentuated her figure; a few inserted godets and panels barely changed her contour.

The man on the other hand, at least the dandy, obtained a

curious silhouette in the fourteenth century. The hosier made legwear for him that fitted his legs very closely, and ended at the toe in a long point. The tailor (who belonged to a different guild) cut the tunic in rounded sections, giving the wearer a very unmasculine shape. Now the time for 'adding on' had arrived for the man, for between the topfabric and the lining of this tunic the tailor stuffed a lot of padding until his client achieved a shape nature never bestowed on him. The girdle, which in past centuries gathered the loose garment around his waist, became superfluous and descended as an ornament around the hips. This is clearly noticeable on the men in the foreground of Plate 7 who are carrying food to the royal and clerical guests.

12. Peasant with apron and padded upper-sleeves. Grimani Breviary. c.1500.

The labourer, however, and the peasant working in the field could not move around sufficiently in such tight clothes. Furthermore a thick and padded layer would be hot and uncomfortable. The working man let his stockings down to prevent breaking the thongs or laces that tied them to his belt. He worked in his shirt and drawers, covered with a loose tunic if necessary. He wore sturdy, coarse shoes or wooden soles tied over his hose.

13. Peasant woman with apron and bodice laced over her shift. Grimani Breviary. c.1500.

The woman's silhouette changed at this time only in so far as her *stance* changed—she leaned backward with abdomen pushed out; a wide, high girdle, which narrowed the waist and at the same time supported the breast, accentuated the stomach even more. The custom of pressing the heavy folds of the woollen, often fur-lined overgown high against the body reinforced this 'line'.

It is not known whether any artificial padding was used to reinforce the silhouette. Probably not: fashion had a pronounced masculine character and would retain this for centuries to come. The man's costume set the style, the woman's followed suit. A woman was 'merely' a woman and aside from some lacing at the waist could not expect too many artifices in her clothing. The enormous hats and coifs were excessive even for a creature who, according to the church's edicts, had no soul.

14. The medieval slouching stance. St Helena. Xanten Cathedral. c.1200.

Just as the woman, with a few exceptions, will always strive for a small waist, the male fashions return again and again to this day to the artificial broadening of the shoulders.

15. This man fills the space between his hose and tunic with his shirt. Italy, 2nd half fifteenth century.

For that purpose, at the end of the fifteenth century, men placed pads on the upper arm, the so-called 'mahoitres'. How they were made and how they were attached is not known. That they were commonly worn and served to support the full sleeves is clearly visible in many pictures. Class distinction also plays a role here: the peasant does not wear them, although he sometimes ties a piece of string around his upper arm, so that his shirt sleeves will puff. The executioners, who were frequently depicted in the fifteenth century, were of too lowly a station to participate in such a fad. Until the advent of photography, we generally know more about the clothing of the well-to-do, who had enough money to have his portrait painted. He had that done maybe once in his lifetime, dressed in his Sunday-best suit and with borrowed

16. French miniature. Fifteenth century.

jewellery. About the clothes of the 'common man' we are less well informed, although the executioners, who made themselves comfortable at their sinister, heavy work by removing their outer garments, provide us with an opportunity to have a look at male underwear.

The *codpiece* (French: *braquette*) would not belong in a discussion of the history of changes of the human body, were it not that the flattening of the loin region, through the ever longer and tighter hose, and the stuffing of the codpiece did alter the man's body-line. How the space between the two separate hose was filled, whether the shirt was tucked inside, or whether the under-drawers filled this gap, did not become an issue until 1450. The tunics had been so long that that part of the body was always covered. The man had enough freedom of movement, while for his bodily functions the drawers were vertically split and then overlapped. But when in the middle of the century the tunics became so short that all the tucked-in underwear became visible it was a sloppy sight indeed! A flap had to be invented to cover it all—and so it was. The flap and the hose had many small holes along the edge, and with narrow tapes the gap was laced.

The hose which by now were sewn in one, middle front and middle back, also had small holes at the waist (usually nine: two on either side in front, two at each sideseam, and one in the middle-back). These corresponded with eyelets in the tunic's waist. Consequently, dressing and undressing was a laborious business: it is curious that the button closing which was used so much in the fourteenth century was now completely forgotten again. At times the man wore dark coloured 'bathing trunks' (which can be observed in pictures of bath-house scenes) underneath the hose, making the use of a flap superfluous.

The codpiece fits entirely in this era, when fashion was provocatively masculine and art had a strong structural character. The knight wore a codpiece of metal attached to his armour, in order to protect his genitals. The burgher followed this fashion later. He wore a flap made of cloth or leather, stuffed, stiffened and, later still, decorated with ornaments. In Germany a bow was tied through it on occasion. The armour's metal codpiece was supplied with a hinge at the top, so that it could be raised for the purpose of urinating. Peasants wore this flap well into the seventeenth century, tied with laces, but no longer stuffed or adorned. This can be observed in the paintings of Brueghel and Jan Steen.

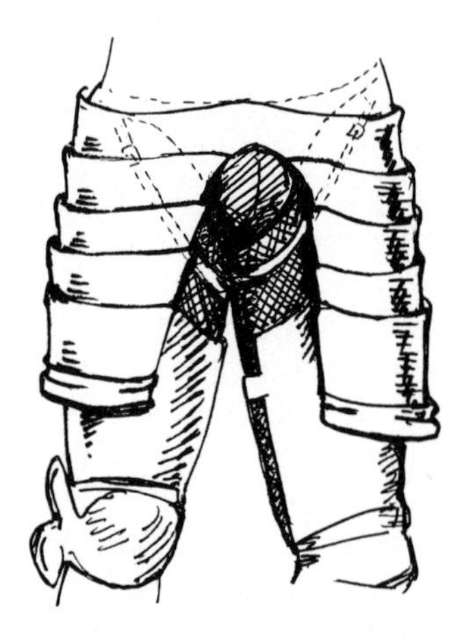

17. Codpiece in armour. Painting in Darmstadt Museum.

8 The Renaissance

(1500–1615)

The sixteenth century was an exuberant time: a time to 'eat, drink and be merry, for tomorrow we die', which possibility was indeed considerable now that wars over religion were raging everywhere and epidemics of pestilence devastated entire towns and villages. It was a time of festivity, of fairs, weddings, guild parades, bath-houses, gardens of love, of courts with splendour-loving kings and their courtesans, such as Henry VIII, Francis I, Charles V, and, in Rome, some joy-loving Popes.

18. Samson and Delilah: Lucas Cranach. Mauritshuis, The Hague. 1st half sixteenth century.

The woman

It is difficult to describe in brief women's dress in the first half of this century, between 1500 and 1550; it was different everywhere, in every country, and in Germany in every town even. Peasant women worked in the field in laced bodices which supported the bust. Rich ladies laced the bodices of their gowns over a beautifully decorated tucker; in some regional costumes they are still laced over a red baize bib.

In this exuberant time women did not need to be prudish: an unabashed *décolleté* was permitted and some hair was even allowed to be shown at times. Thanks also to the fashion of slashed fabrics the chemise was allowed to show through here and there. With the help of magnificent Italian pattern books, the chemise was now enriched with fine, web-like embroidery. Out of these open stitches lace gradually developed.

These fashions could not be considered unwholesome—nothing was 'added', nothing was 'pared away'. There may have been the chance of catching a cold or pneumonia because of the low necklines, but through the ages women have rejoiced in low *décolletages* and have worn them literally with contempt for death. At that time they could at least avail themselves of little shoulder capes to cover the bared bosom. The only thing 'added' consisted of a few additional petticoats: the gown was now always horizontally divided between skirt and bodice, and a bouffant skirt always provided a beautiful contrast to a tight bodice.

The man

Men led women in the display of ostentatious, picturesque clothing which the ladies more modestly followed. Clothes reached extremes: from the scholars' sober black garments (Erasmus, Luther, Moore, and Penn) to the most colourful and fantastic suits of the German Landsknechten which were full of sashes, trimmings and embroidery. Many artists designed and sketched clothes for nobility, burghers, and participants in the many parades.

19. Portrait of a young man by G. Stretes. Hampton Court. 1st half sixteenth century.

The broadening of the shoulders continued. Through the use of big puffed sleeves in the doublet as well as in the short full coat (which in addition had wide lapels) considerable width was achieved. This challenging, stalwart effect was strengthened still further by a large cocked beret, to which, depending on rank and station, jewels or feathers were attached. A pipe or a spoon might even be stuck through a slit in the brim.

The time of the super-refined long pointed shoes was past; the man now had flat, broad shoes, which provided plenty of space for the toes. The smooth narrow hose no longer belonged in this era either: it was divided horizontally at the knee. Above were wide trunk-hose, full of trimmings, puffs and slashes. Under the knee a better cut made the stockings fit more smoothly. Only occasionally were they knitted at this time.

1550–1600

Every period is in fact a reaction to the previous one, but in this instance the contrast is particularly great.

The Spanish court was rich and powerful and hence set the tone. There, Phillip II, not a very cheerful character at best, was living in a sombre palace, built in the shape of a grating in memory of the slow torture death of St Laurentius. The only diversion for the court ladies was an occasional *auto-da-fé*, when they were allowed to witness the burning alive of heretics.

The woman

No wonder that the fashion became stiff and dark. The woman had to be covered from chin to foot, and even further for no foot must be visible. Her shape (in so far as she was permitted to have one) was blurred by stuffing between lining and outer fabric. In a time when people did not wash (that was forbidden: one had to care for one's soul, not for one's body) perspiration could not evaporate under this thick layer; vermin thrived there abundantly. The bosom was a shape absolutely forbidden to women. The devil had placed it on the female body; it had to be hidden or its development prevented. It is said that in the corsets of little girls pieces of lead were bound in the place where breasts ought to grow. It is very likely a true story: little children were always tightly swaddled so the transition from bindings to corset was not great. Babies on the island of Marken wear laced bodices to this day, but thanks to pressure from medical authorities they are now so supple as to be harmless. Very few pictures of children exist from this 'Spanish' era. A daughter of Phillip II peers timorously above a gown stretched tightly over a cuirass. She is completely flat and will probably remain so. Children's clothes did not exist. Little boys as well as little girls were dressed like small women. Only after boys reached the age of five or six was there a festive change-over from skirt to trunk-hose, which turned them into little gentlemen. Little gentlemen they were, with all the accessories: later those would be wigs, brocaded vests and side-swords.

The peasant women wore a stiffened dickey with a ruff, to fill in the *décolleté* of her laced bodice (or a jacket closed with hooks and eyes). The dickey was tied under the armpits, which gave it a stiff Spanish look, but did not cause any discomfort. But lo, the poor lady of distinction! She now started to wear all those laced bodices and chemises *under* her gown: the corset is in the process of development, the corset which she is going to be squeezed into willy nilly from now on. The corset henceforth determines the 'line' of fashion, except for a few 10-year intervals, and the women willingly comply. The first real and especially flattening corset was evidently made by an armourer: it had hinges at the side and hooks in the back. Blacksmiths also constructed the metal framework which supported the stiffly extended farthingale, or *vertugadin*. Around 1500 the farthingale became drum shaped and was called *vertugadin au tambour*.

An ever increasing number of stays were put inside the corset, which were made of strong pliable wood, bone, ivory, or metal and, since the start of whaling, of whalebone.

The man

The man too wore the sombre Spanish fashions which accorded with the atmosphere of those times, Calvin's church-state Geneva, and the centres of the serious minded Huguenots. The doublet was stiff, dark, and stuffed between lining and outer fabric. A high collar with a white ruff forced the neck into a proudly erect stance. The broadening of the shoulders was stylized into a high roll around the armhole. The body line became shorter and fuller, so full in fact that chair seats had to be widened. As a result it became important to emphasize the leg. Nothing is known of the use of false calves and false thighs but beautiful (preferably knitted) silk stockings were much sought after luxury items. They were offered as presents to noblemen and gratefully accepted.

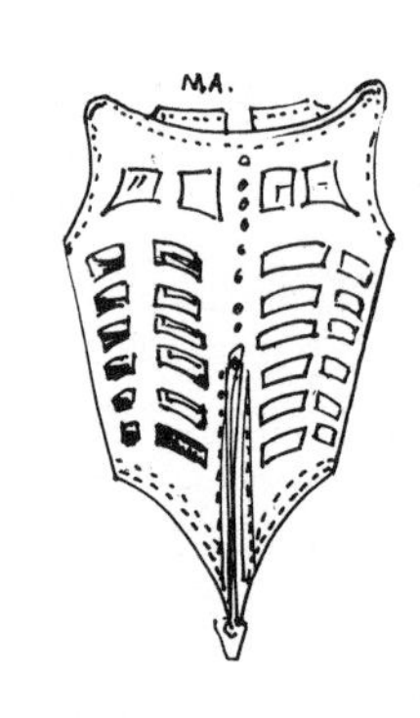

20. Iron corset. Museum Cluny, Paris. Sixteenth century.

The codpiece became smaller and gradually disappeared for several reasons:

a) It all but vanished between the balloon-shaped pant legs.
b) It was barely visible below the peasecod-belly, or below

the basque or roll, which was frequently attached to the doublet's low waist.

c) The art of tailoring showed an unprecedented growth; many new patterns were invented and recorded in famous patternbooks. Now one could assemble the separate sections of pants into one article of clothing. The Spanish tailors were the masters of the trade; the Dutch who fought the Eighty Years' War of liberation against the Spaniards nevertheless copied their patterns carefully.

One of the most curious changes in the male figure is for certain the 'peasecod-belly', made immortal by Punch. One wonders how this peculiar pointed belly, stuffed with flax or hemp pluckings, was arrived at. Most likely its origin is to be found in armour. The armourer welded the two side sections of the breast cuirass together in the middle front. This created a rounded shape at a location where it did not fit the body. Gradually this bulge, as well as the point of the waist, moved downward. The invention of gunpowder made the use of

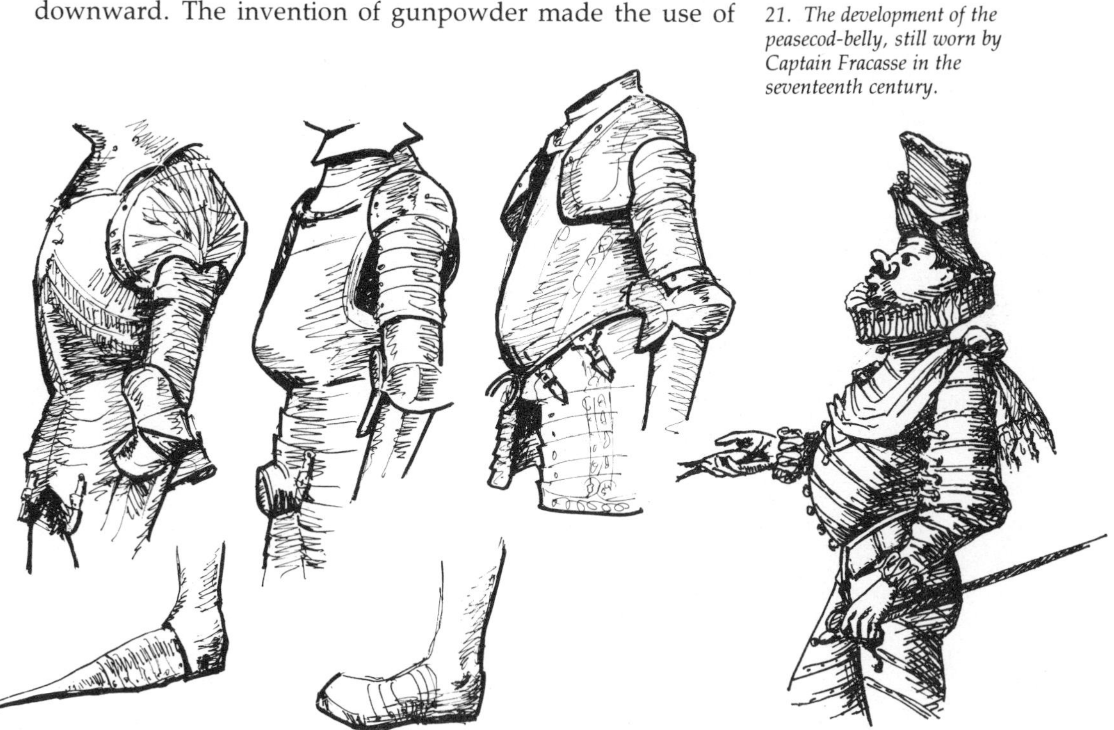

21. The development of the peasecod-belly, still worn by Captain Fracasse in the seventeenth century.

armour superfluous: fighting was done from a distance with guns and cannons. But the fops of that time did not want to relinquish this quaint silhouette, particularly not at a time when a vain king Henri III of France (1574–1589) led the way in the wearing and designing of outlandish clothes. In France, Captain Fracasse was the symbol of a poverty-stricken braggart: he acted very importantly, but held in his hand his midday meal: two scrawny carrots. The peasecod-belly rage lasted about half a century; after 1625 it was no longer seen.

22. Dancing peasant couple. D. Vinckboons. Mauritshuis, The Hague. Seventeenth century. As in the fifteenth century their clothes are still fastened with tapes and laces.

23. Don Juan of Austria.

(1615–1715)

24. Willem van Heythuysen. Frans Hals. Museum of Fine Arts, Brussels. c.1640.

From a fashion point of view the seventeenth century did not begin with the year 1600—a new style and a new 'line' did not develop until about twenty years later.

Life became more cheerful and exuberant. The influence of the sombre, bigoted, pious Spanish court disappeared with Phillip II; Galvin and his severe church-state pressed his stamp less emphatically on north-western Europe; in the Netherlands rest returned at first through the Twelve Years' Armistice and later came a recovery from all the sadness, poverty, and care of the Eighty Years' War, although that did not officially come to an end until 1648. In about 1620 came the transition from the severely symmetrical Renaissance to the billowing forms of the Baroque. Everything had to be round and thick: the columns of buildings, ball-feet under chests, men's pants and women's skirts and sleeves. Around these full sleeves the woman now tied a ribbon, so that she had two billows on each arm.

The man

The man's clothing had a swaggering, military, and purposely careless character at that time; he would walk into a salon in riding boots, and a baldric without powder horns, wearing his large-brimmed felt hat cocked, and showing his underwear here and there through a bit of unbuttoning. His silhouette was a natural one, the shoulder rolls shrank to a narrow band around the armhole, then disappeared for centuries. No stuffing of flax or hemp between lining and outer fabric hid or flattened his body's shape.

This purposely sloppy way of dressing is frequently seen in men's fashions, particularly after wars and revolutions. After the French Revolution fops ordered their tailors to put the wrong pleats in coats and pants, while their hair had to hang down unpowdered in wisps on their shoulders. After the First World War the trench-fashions appeared, with trench coats, puttees, etc. In 1970 hippies frayed the bottoms of their blue-jeans, spot-bleached them with chlorine bleach and disliked nothing more than kempt hair.

The woman

Each epoch has its own female beauty ideal. Around 1620 people had had enough of flat stiff dolls in clothes pulled tightly over metal rods. Although not every peasant woman or toiling burgher dame may have achieved that shape, it does not change the female ideal at the time of the Spanish fashions. In the Baroque era the plump, chubby models as they were painted by Rubens and Jordaens were preferred.

How did women obtain the rounded forms of this new 'line'? In the first place by eating a lot. With Holland's 'Golden Age' came much prosperity; not the least through trade with the Indies. This prosperity was manifest not only through beautiful houses and gardens but also through abundant meals. Never has the art of painting concentrated on depicting food as it did at that time. Those who want to gain some insight into this should one day skip a meal and visit museums where seventeenth-century Dutch paintings are on display. It will make their mouths water. In the kitchen of Gerard Douw a woman is cleaning a stout green cabbage which is going to be filled with juicy minced meat! . . . The hares painted by Jan Weenix . . . think of these served in a cream sauce . . . We observe the repasts of Jan Steen, the frail

25. This woman, painted by Moreelse, shows the rounded forms of the Baroque period. Mauritshuis, The Hague.

little women of Terborg, who pass their admirers those tall glasses of wine; yes indeed wine, that was still missing from the menu. There are paintings of kitchen scenes where portly matrons attack vast supplies of delicacies, enough to feed an orphanage. And let us not forget the still lives, the juicy lemons dripping on pearly white oysters for an epicure's banquet.

The observer of all these culinary delights will now understand that at the time the 'line' was round, natural, and plump, and no thought was given to any paring down. The bodices which were worn as corsets under the dresses, and short jackets, were loosely laced; they did not have to push away anything, nor flatten any bosoms. Only one odd instance of paring occurred in the woman's face, under the cheekbone. The caps were no longer tied under the chin but were sewn to a silver brace, which had a little ball at the end, pressing a small dimple into the cheek. In regional costumes this brace grew larger in succeeding centuries to the wide 'ear-iron', which for example on the island of Urk, Netherlands, still pressed into the cheek. The ordinary woman covered her head less and less with starched caps: she let her hair fall freely in ringlets at the sides, and lightly covered her forehead with a thin fringe, something that was strongly disapproved of by priests and ministers.

26. Eleonora of Bourbon wears the drum-shaped farthingale as she dances with Philips Willem of Orange in 1607. Mauritshuis, The Hague.

Female forms were further accentuated by the wearing of ample clothes made of beautiful heavy fabrics. The shoulders were broadened with two or three starched collars on top of each other, and the hips were given the rounded shape the Baroque fashions prescribed. The latter was no longer done by soldering an iron hoop at hip height to the bottom of the iron corset in order to make the skirt fall over it at a 90 degree angle but the desired shape was achieved by tying a thickly stuffed roll (not surprisingly called a 'sausage') with two strings under the top skirts, on top of the abdomen.

Corsets were always made by men; at first by blacksmiths, later on by corsetiers. In 1675 guilds of 'wool-and-linen-seamstresses' were founded; they were allowed to assist in the making of corsets, but it remained a man's job. Perhaps men did not want to deprive themselves of the pleasure of the fittings. Those became the subject of more or less spicy, satirical prints: the woman stares modestly into space while the corsetier measures, feels, and gropes to his heart's content and the husband watches and gnashes his teeth.

27. The hip-roll, a kerchief and a tiara-cap are lying on a bedroom floor. J. de Brunes.

It has been claimed that the seventeenth-century woman, proud and happy to be pregnant, chose to have her portrait painted with this swelling figure. (It does seem improbable that a woman of that time would crave another pregnancy especially after one child had died in infancy, despite the care of dry nurses, who would with their thumbs push strong

28. *Satirical print of hip-rolls and masks. 1610.*

broth and thick pap down the little ones' throats.) The printer Plantijn in Antwerp distributed congratulatory cards, which wished in beautifully printed letters '. . . much prosperity, few children!'

Yet children had a better chance of survival at this time than in the previous century: the babies one can observe in the paintings of the Dutch school of interiors and maternity rooms are no longer swaddled completely but can move their arms freely.

Second half of the seventeenth century: the man

Around 1660 a time of comfort set in, with much prosperity, and the dominant influence in Europe was the court of Louis XIV. Men's clothing was at first ample and sloppy with lots of lace, neckbands and ribbon loops, until around 1680 several costume elements were combined into a costume-unit that still exists today. It consisted of a shirt, pants, vest, and coat. The shirt was made of linen or silk; for common use cotton was not imported from the tropics until later. Lice felt very much at home in woollen underwear! Only around 1880 did the wearing of woollen undershirts and under-drawers run parallel with the propaganda of the reform movement for personal hygiene.

It is no wonder, then, that the French court enjoyed the stories about King-Stadtholder William III. On his wedding

29. This gentleman shows the wide sloppy costume of the late baroque (notice the ribbon-loops) G. Netscher. Mauritshuis, The Hague.

30. The French dauphin, 'adorned' with wig, gold braid, lace and feathers. Fashion book c.1696. E. Canter Cremers collection.

night he refused the customary strip-tease into a silk night shirt with lace trimmings and stepped into the bridal bed in *woollen* underwear with the announcement that his spouse just would have to get used to it.

The man's silhouette changed constantly in the seventeenth century, but nothing was ever 'added' or 'pared' away. The fashion interest concentrates more on details: lace, jewels, falling bands, cravats, hose, gaiters, canions (knee ruffles), bows on the shoes, feathers on the edge of tricorns, wigs . . . Hair and wigs were subject to many changes, but they were always long and would remain so till about 1800. These expensive wigs were mentioned in wills: 'To my nephew X, I bequeath my wig.' The other members of the family, jealous of this important legacy, maintained that the wig had 'more years than hairs'. It strikes us as even more peculiar that someone would bequeath 'my handkerchief' (singular): that handkerchief was trimmed with gold lace and tassels so could not be washed anyway; therefore one sufficed. Little was visible of the body under all this finery, so that it was not worthwhile changing anything for the sake of a 'line'. The costliness of all these accessories contributed to let the costume serve in maintaining rank and standing. All this demonstrative luxury roused the anger of the champions of a pious, humble life style: the Quakers, Puritans, Baptists, and Huguenots. They dressed uniformly in grey, brown, or black cloth, with falling bands of linen, without lace or blue starch.

31. Woman of c.1665 with long and high corset. P. de Hooch. Collection J. S. Bache, New York.

Second half of the seventeenth century: the woman

The exuberantly rounded forms of the Baroque made way now for the finer lines of the French Louis XIV style.

The silhouette became more slender, without hip rolls; the torso seemed long, through the wearing of corsets which pushed the waist down and the bust up. The dress bodice was pulled tightly, and had in the middle front a sturdy busk of wood, bone, iron, or (when the whaling trade increased) whalebone. It was trimmed with buckles or a row of small bows and was laced in the middle back, and that was the start of a lot of trouble! The girl and the young woman attempted what had not been done for almost half a century: the tight lacing of their waist until it was smaller than their friend's.

32. Baroque again; wide sleeves, soft coiffure. C. Terborch. Mauritshuis. c.1654.

And if mamma or the maid refused to pull the laces any tighter she could do it herself with additional lacing in front! The heavy boning of the dress bodice (in addition to the busk), rendered a corset underneath superfluous. The long pointed waist could destroy the balance between bodice and skirt, therefore the skirt was elongated by a train. A contemporary English letter reads: '. . . girls ought to be wiser . . . they lock their ribcage in a jail, a jail of irons and stays, but they open the door wide to consumption.'

33. Gown, laced over 'planchette'. Metropolitan Museum, New York, c.1690.

As the seventeenth century came to an end, there existed only one centre for all art, culture, and fashion: the court of Louis XIV in Versailles. Tall stately court ladies sat on comfortable high-backed chairs—if indeed they were of a rank high enough to be allowed to sit. How does a woman grow taller in an age when plastic surgery consisted at best of bleeding and the cutting away of lumps of fat, and when there was no question of the artificial lengthening of limbs? She cannot become taller, but she can appear taller. What artifices were used to make a woman seem taller?

34. Courtlady in negligée. Her corset is richly trimmed with lace. Gravure by G. Valck, 1694.

a) The bodice became longer and narrower still, pulled tight from neck to waist; in the triangular opening the 'planchette' or stomacher was visible, made of quilted embroidery, or silk covered with lace or bows. Just as the peasant maiden laced her bodice over a piece of red baize, so the worldly lady laced her bodice over a stomacher. The smooth narrow shoulders also served to make the body appear taller.

b) A tall flounce was attached to her lace cap which, supported with wire stood up straight, with the hair piled high against it in front, and a cluster of ribbon bows in the back. With this cap, called *Fontange*, a woman could add 30 cm to her height.

c) By wearing high heeled shoes she thereby restored the balance between the length of bodice and skirt. In general women wore high heeled shoes when the bodices of their dresses became longer; the time of totally flat shoes, from 1790 till 1845, coincided, therefore, with the high waisted fashions.

35. The duchess of Nevers with a Fontange. Gravure by G. Valck, 1696.

Lengthening of the skirt was desired, since short legs were commonly considered to be a shortcoming. High heels also kept the feet further removed from the dirt in the street: the

36. *Shoes that lengthen the silhouette:*
1. 'clapper-shoe'; the heel is detached from the sole.
2 and 3. Shoes from 1700. Bally Museum, Schönenwerd, Switzerland.

heel flattered the foot, made the instep appear higher, making the woman walk less energetically, which created a more dependent and helpless impression, causing her hips to swivel more, while the too small shoes roused feelings of pity and protectiveness. The uncomfortable gait of high heeled women is therefore a strong stimulant to the opposite sex.

One of fashion's most important functions is to demonstrate and maintain class distinction. The working woman and the peasant toiling in the field cannot afford to be uncomfortably shod. This is most clearly shown in China where formerly the slaves had large feet, while ladies had 'bound' tiny feet. Now that everybody works in modern China, the slow tottering walk of deformed feet no longer makes any sense. The stimulation of the opposite sex does not fit their present system of population restriction through late and voluntary marriages.

d) A still longer train helped to elongate the entire silhouette: this train, worn over a beautifully decorated petticoat, was pulled backward in puffs and draperies. In support of this draped train there appeared an appliance which will be mentioned many more times in this study of the body's 'line': it is the *queue de Paris* (Parisian tail). This was a padding made of gummed linen, which caused the train to fall more gracefully and, by contrast, flatter the straightness of the back and the hollow in the loins. The sides of this

37. Two children c.1700. Hearth figures in the museum Bisdom van Vliet in Haastrecht.

draped train also needed some support and it appears that for this purpose false hips could be purchased.

This 'line' remains till 1715. With the death of Louis XIV the influence of his secret spouse Mme de Maintenon, who put a stamp of pious virtue on the court, also vanished. A never explained peculiarity of that era was the large number of transvestites. A nephew of the English Queen Anne, the governor of New York from 1702 till 1708, dressed in his aunt's clothes. Another military man, the knight of Eon, marched before his troops in long, trailing gowns, rattling his sabre. Queen Christina of Sweden dressed in men's clothes.

10 Rococo

(1715–1790)

There are two moments in history when man discovered the joys of life on earth! The first was at the end of the fifteenth century, when Charles VIII of France (1483–1498) marched his armies to Italy (to settle a conflict of succession) and found beauty and refinement, and a culture devoted to pleasure such as was unknown in the austere medieval castles of France. The second moment was after the death of Louis XIV in 1715, when 'rococo' arrived—a collective name for all that is charming, refined and comfortable! People no longer lived in chilly halls of state but in small, comfortable salons. Chairs were upholstered with heavy cushions; all furniture served man's ease and pleasure; one ate and drank out of egg-shell thin porcelain; the cut of clothes improved, fabrics were softer, wigs were small and always powdered white.

38. Drawing by Gravelot, c. 1730.

First half of the eighteenth century: the man

In this time of much gaiety and little prudery, the man did not always have to demonstrate his standing and his dignity. Fashion's main influence was now more the woman's dress, and men's clothes were influenced by it. Soft colours, much

39. The servant laces his obese master's corset. Early nineteenth century.

embroidery, and many lace flounces were used. Even his waist was laced in by corsets, to create an elegant contrast to the widely spread skirt of his coat. There was no shoulder padding as sturdy, broad, masculine shoulders were the last thing a rococo fop desired.

Coat and vest became shorter and the lower part of the legs were clearly visible. They were no longer covered by tall boots, or frills at the knee, the so-called 'canions'. The unfortunate man who could not show off beautiful muscular calves had to resort to buying a false pair in the store, and wear them underneath his stockings.

40. Gentleman with corset and false calves. Etching by Lewis Mark, c.1800.

The advantages and disadvantages of this padding was nowhere discussed more plainly than in the memoires of Captain Coignet, which he set down in his old age (*Les cahiers du Capitaine Coignet*, Hachette). In 1809 he entered Paris with Napoleon's army; to his great joy he was promoted to the rank of sergeant and earned 43 sous a day. But with the higher rank came two added duties: he had to learn to write, and he was obliged to wear white silk stockings. Unfortunately, however, a cloud darkened his happiness: he had no

Plate 1. (*opposite*) Cretan priestess in leather bodice. Decorated earthenware statuette, c.1700 B.C.

Plate 2. (*above*) The fair nymph Calypso gives provisions to the departing Odysseus. Note the high bust.

calves. He had to wear false paddings, which frankly he disliked. His problem required an instant solution, for he received an invitation to attend a feast at his captain's, where he would meet many beautiful ladies. He went to the Palais Royale (then a centre for amusement, shops, and restaurants) and bought a pair of under hose, the pads (which cost 18 francs a pair—one had to make sacrifices for the sake of beauty), a second pair of stockings to smooth out the edges of these pads, and finally the white silk over-stockings.

At the feast he sat between two beautiful, sophisticated ladies, who were noticeably impressed by this dashing sergeant. The following morning, the chambermaid of the most charming of the ladies arrived with an invitation for a rendezvous. On the wings of love he hastened to the indicated address. The maid organized everything: he had to wait as first she must undress madame before he could go into the bedroom. As he entered, madame awaited, in a magnificent bed . . . But what about him? Was he in the throes of love's delirious intoxication? Not at all. He could think only of his false calves and the difficulty of divesting himself of three pairs of stockings. With much effort he succeeded in smuggling the calves underneath his pillow, which however did not make for a restful slumber. The following morning madame left him tactfully alone for a moment so that he could hastily get dressed in private.

Back in the barracks his friends asked, 'What is wrong with your stockings? You look as if you are wearing false calves.' He immediately removed the costly paddings and tossed them in the fire: 'From now on it is spindle-shanks for me.' P.S. The romance did not last.

Padded calves and waist-corsets remained a part of the man's wardrobe through the entire eighteenth and part of the nineteenth centuries.

In the second half of the eighteenth century man's dress became more sober, lost the flair and the elegance, such as the small waist of the full-skirted coat, the wide cuffs, the lace frills. His clothes became tighter, darker, narrower. The wigs were merely stiff rolls. At this time, fashion was influenced by England, where a rural culture prevailed over the urban one, and practical clothes were worn for sports and hunting.

41. Bodices.
1. laced in front. Loose sleeves.
2. laced in the back.
3. laced in front over fichu.

42. Underwear for sale at the market in doll's town.
1. Corset, laced in back.
2. Petticoat with Brussels' lace.
3 and 4. Bust paddings of quilted embroidery.

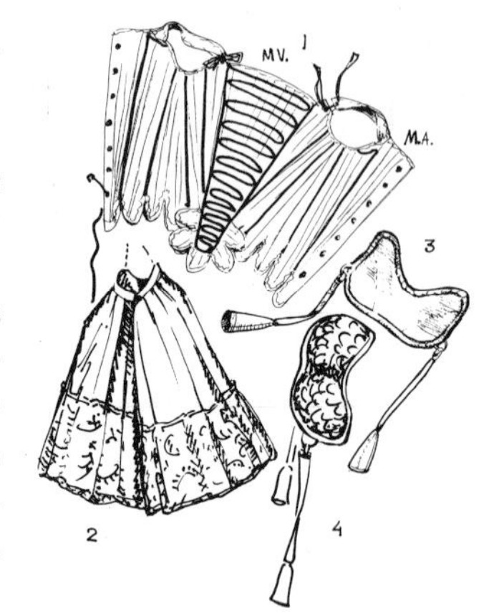

First half of the eighteenth century: the woman

Never had fashion's 'line' been more beautiful, more charming, more graceful than in the eighteenth century, and never, except perhaps around 1900, had eroticism played such an important role. Certainly, around 1660–1680, ladies displayed a bold *décolleté*, but its cleverly subtle effect was not as striking as the demonstration of dignity and class distinction of the gentlemen. And furthermore these bare throats and bosoms were openly on view; nothing was veiled, nothing was left to the imagination and a man's eye was soon sated with all this display of bare flesh. Just as in our time, after all the hot pants, and mini skirts, the man has had his fill of women's legs—beautiful, ugly, fat, or skinny. It will be a long time before a girl can get a reaction from a man by displaying the tip of her foot at a ball by making it appear stealthily from under the skirt as a result of some clever knee shuffling. For that matter it will be a long time before the sight of a lady's shoe will make her dancing partner blush.

The bare throat of the rococo lady could only be discovered with some difficulty among all the lace trimmings of chemise, corset and dress, plus ruchings around the neck, and was in addition tenderly covered with thin batiste fichus. This applied to the dress of the chamber maid and peasant as well; they too covered the *décolleté* with a fichu, which had a tendency to shift, offering the suitor a short-lived glance at the fair skin. In Haydn's famous oratorio *The Seasons* one can hear how Hannah spins and weaves her fichu. Naturally those bosoms were not always full enough to cause the essential swelling underneath the fichu. To combat such deficiencies industry provided extensive padding for busts, as well as for calves and thighs. These paddings can be seen in the famous dolls' houses in Arnstadt, East Germany, where Princess Augusta Dorothea von Schwarzburg-Arnstadt (1666–1751), with the help of all the artisans on her estate, and with the cooperation of her spiritual advisers (two Franciscan priests), built 26 miniature doll houses, where in 84 rooms 411 dolls were housed. Eighteenth-century life in miniature can be observed there in its entirety. The paddings are lying on a chair in a bedroom, and are for sale in stalls in the market place. They are covered on top with quilted embroidery. The

Plate 3. Relief showing Romans in togas.

Plate 4. (*opposite*) Nobles clad in fabrics woven in Byzantine silk.

function of hooked-on bands with lead weights is unknown.

The waist

43. Children in cuirasses.

A graceful body was highly valued, heavy and plump at the top, then tapering to an extremely small waist. The shoulders were set back so that the back became straight and flat as it was not proper to have protruding shoulder blades. How was such a figure acquired? By corseting children, especially little girls almost at birth. The philosopher J. J. Rousseau (1712–1778) who strongly advocated a simpler, healthier and more natural way of life loudly opposed this practice. But it was only through the influence of doctor Tronchin, who discovered that fresh air was beneficial to one's health, that a children's corset was created, made entirely of leather and with 'only' three metal stays in it. To walk back and forth on the balcony at his advice was called 'to tronchinate', and very progressive little children were 'cuirassé au Tronchin' (corseted à la Tronchin). The daughters of parents who were so modern that they let their children wear loose garments would not, later on, enter the many beauty contests that added lustre to many festivities. They would not stand a chance of winning a prize for the smallest waist, or the flattest back; nor for the best teeth, something that was very rare at that time. The corset was laced both back and front: it had a row of tabs at the bottom, which fell over the wide petticoat.

The crinoline

Nothing made the waist look smaller than the contrast with skirts extending over petticoats stiffened with horsehair (French: *crin*, hence crinoline). These were of braided rope, or doubly quilted linen, or silk. The 'hoopskirt' did not arrive until a century later when the circumference had to be so large that it could no longer be achieved with a crinoline.

On top of the crinoline a white skirt was worn with a beautiful lace flounce at the bottom; the top skirt went over that. A peasant girl's clothes consisted of a shift, skirts, an apron, hose, garters, and shoes. In addition a jacket was often worn made of a beautifully printed cotton, imported from India and printed locally. Over the petticoat that covered the crinoline a lady wore an ample gown, sometimes a lace apron, and a stomacher that was pinned to the corset in the middle front. And how about drawers? Was there nothing to cover the abdomen and the thighs? Indeed there was not. In Holland maids only wore drawers as they sat on the window sill, wiping the panes. A woman wore white cotton or silk stockings to the disapproval of pious old ladies who considered silk stockings sinful. Whether or not a woman had pretty legs made no difference; except in a few more or less spicy prints, they are not visible.

For Tsarina Elizabeth of Russia (daughter of Peter the Great, predecessor and aunt by marriage of Catherine the Great) this was a pity, because she was proud of her pretty legs. Since she could only show them off in men's clothes she gave many transvestite balls at her 'Winterpalace' in Leningrad. (As one walks through the endless halls of this palace today, now the Hermitage, one can appreciate that there was plenty of room for balls and feasts.) Ladies did not wear false calves, at least they did not appear in the extensive wardrobe of the Russian royal families.

Although foot and shoe were now visible, what was further hidden by the skirts remained a sweet secret. In order to solve that riddle a man could do three things: first of all he could peek when a lady retied her garter around her knee, secondly he could romp with a girl so wildly that she fell down, and finally he could push her as she sat on the swing. Consequently, the swing became a very popular plaything among youngsters. All three situations are frequent subjects of contemporary paintings and prints.

Towards the middle of the century the woman adopted an additional dimension, particularly in her gala dresses: she no longer divided the skirt-fullness evenly around the waist, but placed it exclusively at the hips: she supported this fullness with the so-called 'panniers'. The story goes that a peasant girl going to market tied two baskets under her skirt in order to achieve a handsome figure. Such tales are never true: in the first place no hip padding can be added at a location where the gown makes no allowance for it; secondly, it would pull the skirt up exceedingly at the sides, showing the legs and underwear; in the third place, fashions are never 'invented'—they develop slowly towards their final form.

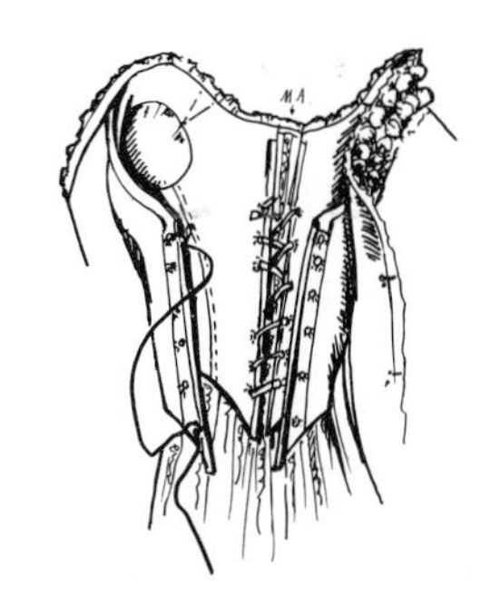

44. Corset sewn inside the dress. National Museum, Copenhagen. c.1770.

45. Crinolines 1 and 2 of braided rope. Hermitage, Leningrad. 3. Quilted oilcloth. Gothenburg Museum.

46. 'After romping'. Painting by W. Hogarth. Fitzwilliam Museum, Cambridge.

Plate 5. (*above*) Doctor and patient. Red hose and white drawers can be seen.

Plate 6. (*below*) The baptism of Charles VI in 1368.

Plate 7. (*opposite*) A banquet at the court of Charles VI.

These wide skirts gave a solemn impression and were worn a great deal at court. Man equated a person's worth with the amount of space he occupied, hence the ample togas for judges, voluminous chasubles and pluvials for the Roman Catholic orthodox high services, long trains for coronation mantles, etc. The space that had to be accorded a woman in panniers was considerable! Carriage doors had to be widened; she could only take a seat in her sedan chair by using collapsible panniers. The wide flat surface of these skirts provided room for much decoration: flower garlands, lace flounces, draperies and heavy solemn embroideries.

As it was agreed that the widening of the hips was not achieved by tying on two baskets the question arises: how was it done? Through the use of all sorts of appliances of reed and bone stretched over grey linen and tied around the waist with a tape. Usually it contained a large pocket, which could be reached through a slit in the skirt. Tapes on the inside

47. Fashion-doll with paniers. c.1760.

could be adjusted at will to regulate the outer curve of the bones. The circumference of the gowns became more modest toward 1775, the broadening of the hips decreased, but the padding was pushed to the rear, where pillows and rolls shaped what would be called a century later the *queue de Paris*. The body obtained a less triangular, more a rectangular look. While pressure on the waist eased somewhat (and therefore on the liver, the stomach, the spleen, and the lower ribs) the entire rib-cage was now stiffly encased in order to push the breast up as high as possible. A sort of pigeon-breast was at that time the fashion ideal, and since no one has such a shape by nature, the high corset helped, together with stiffly starched, puffed-up fichus, which rested on a metal brace that reached from armpit to armpit. These fichus were supposed to move gently up and down with the help of 'sigh machines'. This appliance has not survived in any costume collection. Maybe women were clever enough to feign a 'heaving bosom' without such a device.

The courts, the ladies, the milliners and hairdressers now, however, pounced upon something else: the enormous coiffures and wigs, which gave women a new 'line' and new proportions. People said: 'A woman's head is now in the middle of her body.' Surely an exaggeration, although it is true that a figure did not stop with the head then: an entire length was added to it. When in 1774, after the birth of her first child, Queen Marie Antoinette suffered a loss of hair, wigs became lower and wider. The high wigs had to be dusted with powder every day, using up tons of flour; no wonder that this caused bad blood in times of failing crops, and famine, as it underlined the callous indifference of the aristocracy towards the peasantry (one of the contributing causes of the French Revolution). Class distinctions were very significant. When a rich lady piled her hair high with a mass of gauze, ribbons and feathers, people might shrug their shoulders and say: 'Well, she does not know any better', or 'That's the rich for you!' But for the charwoman, the street singer, the pedlar, or the fishmonger with her pushcart such a hairdo would have been improper. Aside from being out of keeping with their class, it would also have been unhygienic if the powder from the vendor's wig found its way to the

48. Paniers in Nordiska Museum, Stockholm:
1. with pockets on the inside.
2. ditto on the outside.
3. also with back padding.
4. a shorter model.

49. Paniers of stuffed linen with sturdy hoops. 2. lies on top of 1. Closing in back. 3. is built into the petticoat. Nordiska Museum, Stockholm.

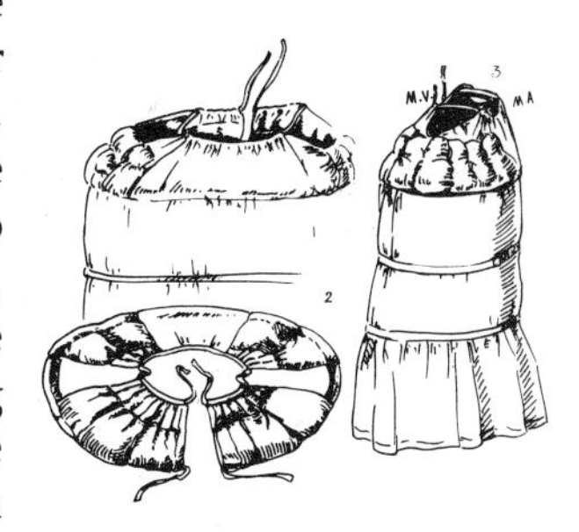

Plate 8. German countrymen in their dashing attire. 1st half sixteenth century.

Plate 9. (*opposite*) This English painting (1588) shows the drum-shaped skirt which was worn over a metal frame.

merchandise.

Class distinction is also known in regional costumes. Fishermen's wives wore one type of cap, but the fleet owner's wife a different one. In the nineteenth century ladies in

50. Caricature of the high wigs. c.1770.

51. 'Departed glory'. Caricature of paniers, wide wigs and make-up. 1783.

Friesland starched the flounce at the back of their lace cap to such a degree that it stood out horizontally. But the servant maid was not allowed to share in this luxury. Her flounce had a limp droop. Since the onset of the use of starch in the second half of the sixteenth century this was a point of great weight and much discrimination, no less so than the question whether the colour of the starch should be yellowish or bluish. It is interesting that all these odd shapes (crinoline, queue, pigeon-breasts) returned exactly a century later.

Fig. 52 from the year 1775 shows on the right a 'polonaise', a gown in which the fullness at the back was horizontally pulled up at the two side-seams. A 'polonaise' is always modestly padded, never has panniers. Around 1880 this horizontal drapery can be observed again in dresses cut without a seam at the waist, and with a moderate bustle. They appear in paintings by Manet, and were popular with older women.

Plate 10. (*above*) Seventeenth-century dress. Frans Hals, Rijksmuseum, Amsterdam, 1637.

Plate 11. (*opposite*) The wide and sloppy clothes of the late baroque. Painting by Pieter de Hooch, Louvre, Paris.

68

11 Empire

(1790–1815)

53. *The deliberate sloppyness of the Merveilleuses and Incroyables. Drawing by Debucourt, c.1795.*

52. (opposite) *'At the opera' around 1775. Notice the wigs, waists and paniers.*

The French Revolution, which had already been smouldering and fermenting for a century, erupted on July 14, 1789 and soon this upheaval reached the other nations of Europe as well. Only Russia had to wait till 1917.

A new time demands a new look. Rococo was a thing of the past, no more luxury, refinement, and eroticism carried to extremes. All this former beauty was tossed overboard: no more precious laces, high heels and powdered wigs, everything must now be unrestrained, loose, and natural. The fops of this era demonstrated their revolutionary persuasion with exaggeratedly sloppy dress. Trousers hung in folds around their legs, vests and coats were too small and too short, the collar much too large, and hair hung in untidy strands around the head: even the cane could not be straight and smooth. The shortness of the vest drew attention to the trouser closing, which was now covered with a flap. These flaps are present to this day in some regional clothes and are worn by those exposed to extreme cold. For instance, the fisherman is protected against the cold sea wind with a belly-band of red baize and a flap on his trousers. When the confused time of

Plate 12. The Duke of Schleswig-Holstein and family. Tischbein, c. 1760.

Plate 13. French engraving. Bibliothèque Nationale, Paris.

transition ceased, however, when clothes were again fitted tightly, and neatly, a new way was sought to smooth this (usually white) space on the abdomen and thighs. In order to achieve this, it was necessary to buy not only false calves, and bust-stuffings for the ladies, but also thigh-pads. A pair of long drawers which are preserved in the costume museum in Bath, England shows furthermore a layer of woollen loops on the inside, in those locations where the male leg requires supplementation.

Trousers became even longer in imitation of those worn by the sailors of Marseilles, who were the first to proclaim the revolution. These long pants became fashionable, and are still with us today. The male costume became even more sobre, darkened and settled into a grey, colourless utility suit, and remained so till about 1960.

Napoleon gave Europe a new appearance: a new court, a new style, and ... wars. Half of Europe's men donned uniforms and fought for, or against, Napoleon. These soldiers had nothing in common with the graceful rococo gentlemen of the previous century: they no longer wanted narrow shoulders and small waists. Gradually the desire for broad shoulders returned. A mess-jacket from 1809, in the army museum in Leyden, is the first one to show a linen interlining covering the chest, but not yet at the back and

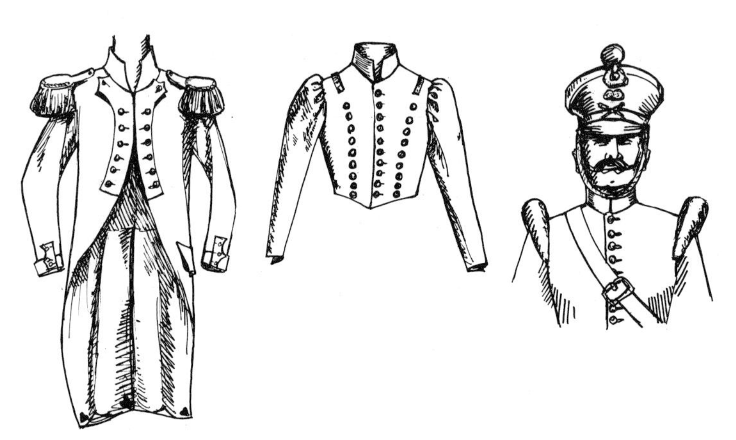

54. Officer's uniform coat of the Batavian Republic (1798). Shoulders broadened by epaulettes; already some chest-padding inside. Army museum, Leyden.

55. Mess jacket of yellow cloth, 1809. No shoulder padding as yet, but fullness in the sleeve's head. Army museum, Leyden.

56. Gunner, shoulders raised with rolls, the so-called 'wings'. Army museum, Leyden, 1831.

shoulders; the head of the sleeve has shirred fullness. A drummer in 1815 and a gunner in 1831 have so-called 'wings' around the armhole. Their superiors soon achieved a sturdy effect through the use of epaulettes.

The woman

Influenced by Rousseau's nature preachings, by the outdoor life in England, and the loose garments found at the excavations in Herculaneum and Pompeii, progressive French ladies had already liberated themselves from corsets, paddings and complicated rococo gowns ten years before the French Revolution. They wore a 'robe chemise' of white lawn: ample fitting, loose and with a ribbon around the waist.

The painter Mme Vigee-le Brun portrays herself with her little daughter in similar Roman attire; Emma Hamilton, the mistress of naval hero Lord Nelson, gives receptions in Naples clad in such draperies, and fashionable Parisiennes pose for portraits dressed in that fashion. Only a few additional strands of hair are required and come the Revolution madame will be dressed for it!

After the most violent years of the Revolution (the 'terreur') had spent themselves and men again wore clothes of proper cut, women also adopted a more form-fitting style. The waist rose higher still and a narrow belt divided a bodice with short sleeves and a very low *décolleté*, and skirt with a long train. The fabric was usually a thin white lawn. There was little room under these dresses for underwear and thus the smooth knitted drawers appeared, which in the twentieth century took their place in fashion as 'directoirs', when around 1910 skirts become too tight to accommodate the customary linen. It is easy to guess that these thinly clad ladies got an earful from their prudish sisters ('the only decent thing are her pink stockings, they are at least blushing about the rest of her clothes'). Initially these Empire fashions degenerated indeed into veritable nudism.

The sudden change from the solid, silken rococo gowns with linings and facings, to the thin, low-cut garments probably resulted in many fatal cases of pneumonia. That was a pity, naturally, but little things like that never change the fashion picture. They might at best prompt people to buy a

57. White cotton under-jacket, the sturdy lining closes with 10 hooks and eyes and supports the bust. Museum Willet, Holthuizen.

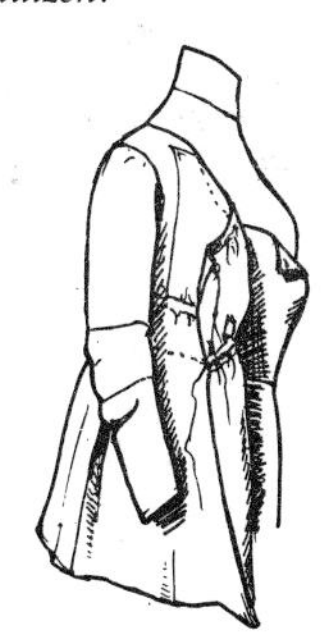

Plate 14. M. and Mme. Lavoisier. Madame is in a 'robe chemise'.
Painting by F. S. Bradford.

Plate 15. A musical evening, c.1830.

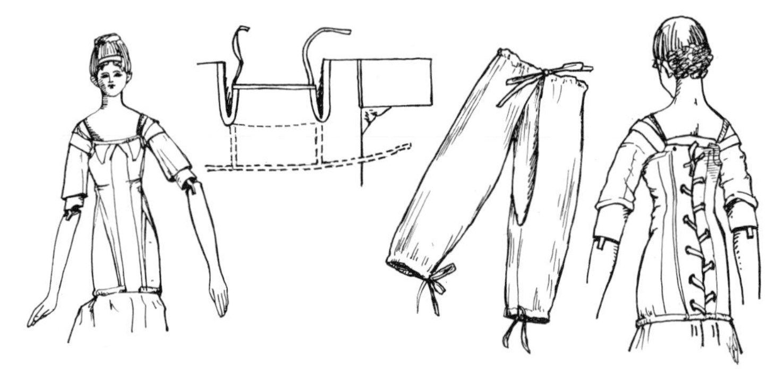

58–61. This doll is from c.1810. (To obtain the low décolleté, the flaps in front and back can be turned down and tied under the armpits.) Under her dress the doll wears a pair of open drawers of ribbed cotton, tied at the calf, two petticoats and a corset that laces in the back.

few additional cashmere shawls.

It was the time of 'liberty, equality, and fraternity', but the equality was not a huge success: in dress there was much class distinction. In the country these fashions were impossible. You cannot milk a cow while you are wearing a white batiste train. The peasant continued to wear the pretty, flattering eighteenth-century clothes, with laced bodice or jacket. This continued to be the basis of all regional wear. The laced

62. Caricature: the lady buys a beautiful false bust.

bodice or the jacket's strong lining supported the bust; the ankle-free skirt and apron were practical for all work in the field. The regional dress did not escape the Empire influence entirely; the waist of peasant bodices also rose.

Between the two extremes of the thin white garment and practical country-wear was the solid dress of a stiff fabric, without a train. It did have the raised waistline, but was high-necked and long-sleeved. Underneath, lingerie was

63. English ladies with pads underneath their beach dresses. Fashion plate, 1897.

Plate 16. A meeting of nineteen inventors. American Gallery, Washington D.C., 1860.

Plate 17. Edward VII and Alexandra of Denmark. Bibliothèque Nationale, Paris, 1905.

worn. A doll of that period shows of what elements that consisted. Her corset is more like a long linen bodice; it gives the figure a 'shape' without pushing anything out of place; that would have been in keeping with a time that clamoured for 'nature', some women's liberation, and extolled 'civic virtue' over the erotic titillations of times past. A lot of padding was indulged in, though. The short bodice demanded a heavy bosom; if nature did not provide it, some stuffing had to be done: a wad of paper, a folded cloth, or artificial breasts, so long as a pronounced roundness provided a strong contrast to the long straight skirt. The lining of the top part of the dress, which was usually laced, produced support for the bust, and pushed it up. Spiteful contemporary commentaries are supplied by Dr Cunnington in his book about underclothes: 'the fashion of false bosoms has at least this utility, that it compels our fashionable fair to wear something.' (From old English letters.)

A quaint and exclusively English stuffing were the 'pads', large flat pillows, which young girls wore under their skirts fore and aft, supposedly in honour of a popular, but pregnant duchess. Cunnington gives us once again a contemporary critique: 'When our grandmothers were pregnant they wore 'jumps' to conceal it. Our modern ladies, who are not pregnant wear pads to carry the semblance of it. From thence it may be inferred our grandmothers had some shame, while their descendants had none!'

The children reaped the benefits from the striving for freedom and naturalness: on the continent they now started to wear simple, loose, children's clothing with bare arms and necks, which their English comrades had already enjoyed for years. Little boys wore a shoulder sash with these English suits, which gave rise to a warning not to get too close to the fire with those loosely flapping clothes. This shoulder sash is still worn occasionally, e.g. by flower pages at weddings. And the warning still makes little children shudder in pity for poor Willy:

Little Willy in his brand new sash
Fell in the fire and was burned to ash.
Later on the night grew chilly
But nobody came to poke poor Willy.

12 Post Empire

(1815–1840)

This period lasted from Napoleon's downfall until the emergence of the constitutional monarchies of 1848. At the Congress of Vienna in 1814, where the crowned heads of Europe gathered, accompanied by their wives and mistresses, to reconstruct the map of Europe, the festive revelry brought about by this occasion interfered with their labours. Beautiful clothes were needed for attendance at all these balls and festivities. Vienna displayed a luxury which was not consonant with the poverty that prevailed in war ravaged Europe. A mere five years was sufficient for Europe to regain its composure after all the wars and changes. The soldiers were either dead or they had abandoned the life of exuberant gratification, and had become respectable family men.

Man had had his fill of 'liberty', and of lusting after scantily clad ladies. As a reaction, virtue and modesty were sought after, and a more artful way of covering the body. For women, these were the days of antimacassars, of embroidering slippers; of great economy, for Europe was impoverished by the wars. Not many clothes have survived from that period: people did not preserve them, but wore them until they were in rags. From those rags little girls made dolls' clothes at the sewing and knitting schools that now proliferated.

Under King Willem I, the Netherlands had a sobre, economy-minded court, which felt little need for expensive gala dress. In this quiet time, with its subdued living-room romanticism, a longing grew for the distant past, and distant lands. The Orient was admired and pictures were created of Bedouins and erupting volcanoes; savage novels were read of times gone by. In England romanticism was reflected in the novels of Sir Walter Scott. In France people grew ecstatic about 'Paul et Virginie', in Germany over 'Werther'. Young men wrote their sweethearts sentimental poems, preferably with a small drawing in an 'Album Amicorum'.

Technology advanced rapidly in this period: many things were invented which we now take for granted such as matches, the sewing machine, oil lamps, steel steamboats, etc. The man who occupied himself with such matters was no longer suited in clothes of silk; only his vest would retain for a long time a modicum of flair and colour. The influence of

64. The fashion. 1820–1830–1840.

65. Fashion for gentlemen and young men. 1840.

women's fashions was even noticeable in men's wear: shoulders did not widen, but sleeves did, the hips too seemed broader as a result of pleats in the pants. The waist had to be small and despite all the advocated simplicity corsets were much in vogue. Who prescribed this simplicity?

66. 'Spindle-shanks'. Drawing by Rudolf Töppfler, 1840.

The famous fops did. In England it was Mr Brummel, the first one to order his shirt collars to be starched, and let the sharp points stand straight upright, thus creating what the Dutch called 'patricides'. The general tendency for well-groomed simplicity came from France's Count d'Orsay; the English statesman Disraeli also set the fashions.

At that time every gentleman wore a top hat; not much 'equality' remained as the ordinary working men wore visor caps. Not even the poorest beggar would go hatless; that would not come about until the end of the nineteenth century when the 'vegetarians' started that trend. Through the emergence of fashion plates, more is known about the clothes of the time. Printing techniques had made great strides and the best artists were engaged in making magnificent lithographs for fashionable magazines. One must remember, however, that the fashion plate always presents an idealized picture; the reality would soon become apparent when photography came into use.

Man of the time was an odd mixture of sentiment and technical know-how; railway stations and factories were built to look like gothic cathedrals and offices to look like temples. A catalogue exists in which samples of ruins can be found to be erected in one's garden. Upon request stuffed owls will be included in the consignment!

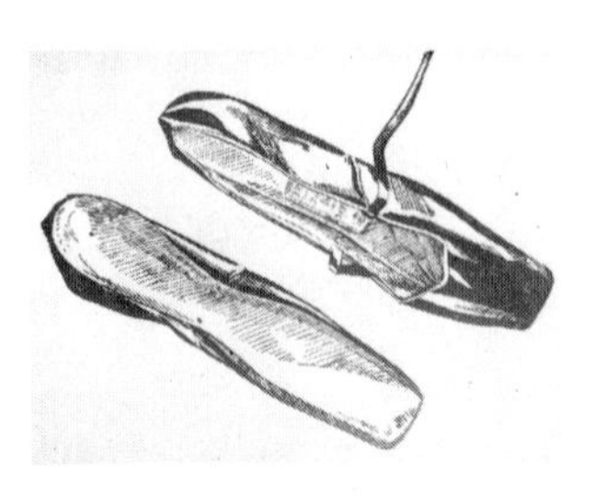

67. Narrow shoes, c. 1830.

The *woman* remained a lowly creature, who softly whispered 'yes'; never said 'no' to father, husband, or brother. Were they really so meek? Of course not, but they had been taught to pretend. Man, in this instance woman, clings stubbornly to her mistakes: she abuses her body and her feet, in spite of all the movements for 'liberty' and 'naturalness'. It is in this century that the maltreatment of the foot begins in earnest: in previous centuries all shoes had been made by hand and to measure. Only as an exception would a cobbler occasionally make up a supply to be sold at the fair. Even the rococo mules provided room for the toes, and the curved heel was well placed under the foot. The trouble began around 1820 with those flat, straight shoes: they had to be equally wide at the toe as at the heel and when the wearer's toes had managed to make a little space after much torture the left shoe was put on the right foot and vice versa in order to 'keep the shoes nice and straight'. The same thing happened with the booties that were becoming fashionable then. But machines for shoemaking were invented. Increasingly shoes were machine-made in factories, and sold in stores; as a result a situation arose where the shoe was not made to conform to the shape of the foot, but the other way around; the foot was supposed to adjust to the shape of the shoe, with the resulting pain, corns, bunions, hammertoes, compressed toes and, consequently, ingrown toe nails.

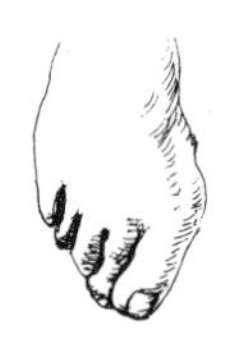

68. Foot of a modern woman, c. 1930. Jubilee book of the Aa-Be factories, Tilburg.

No article of dress exuded such an air of eroticism as the shoe; the reason may be that in the nineteenth century a tip of the shoe was barely visible underneath all those skirts and trains, as a reminder that women, after all, had legs, which was something one hardly dared contemplate in those days.

Footwear would only become visible when, in the process of sitting down, the crinoline would tilt upward, and later, when the train was picked up to reveal the bootie between the flounced petticoats, as in a framework of ribbons, silk and laces. Around 1900 the shoes improved and the so-called 'curved last' arrived; this meant that it was at last realized that humans had a right foot and a left foot!

Although in the twentieth century low-heeled, reform and health shoes were introduced, they were only worn by a small percentage of people. The man wore only whatever the store offered; the woman would not relinquish a means to appear helpless, to reduce the energy of her actions, and to wiggle her hips. A sexy walk is impossible in sturdy sports shoes.

69. The cut-out figures clearly show the family's clothes. Note the leg o' mutton sleeves and the width above and below the tiny waist. As an exception, feet are visible. c.1830.

The heel which had disappeared with the French Revolution returned in the middle of the nineteenth century, but only on ladies' shoes. At this time the tradition was established that shoes had to be too small and must hurt.

The body-line of the wealthy woman of this period changed. Her breasts had been pushed up for so long that she had developed wrinkles near her shoulders; but now they could occupy their normal place, supported by the upper edge of the corset, which suddenly acquired an hour-glass shape. The corset was once again tightly laced to the waist, placed a little lower now, sitting frail and brittle between the

70. Under-bodice with padded sleeves as support for the leg o' mutton sleeve. Platt Hall, Manchester, c.1830.

two large bubbles of the newly filled-out skirt (with a modest bustle-pad in the back, and many starched petticoats), and huge leg o' mutton sleeves. It was fitting in this sentimental, romantic age that the little woman was (or seemed to be) a delicate creature in danger of breaking in half, and thus roused feelings of pity and appealed to the man's protective impulses.

The waist of the 1830 corset, kept in storage at the Hermitage in Leningrad, measures 46 cm. The nana must have

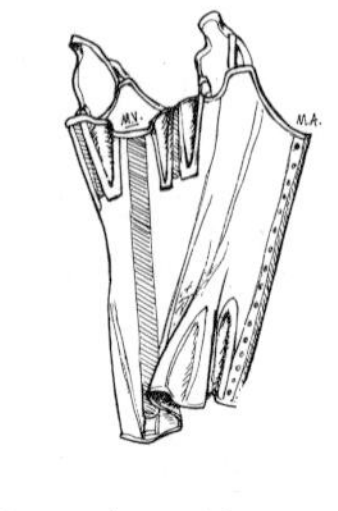

71. Corset for a 46 cm waist. Depot of the Hermitage, Leningrad.

72. Fashion plate showing a young girl's pantalettes. 1853.

pulled very hard at the young lady's laces, for Russian women are in general strongly built and sturdy. (The nana was a dear old slave who took care of rich Russian children and spoiled them.) This lacing was of course very unhealthy, but nobody forced a girl to pull her laces so tightly that her waist was smaller than her girl friend's: it was entirely a voluntary torture.

73. Maid's bodice of printed cotton. She wore no corset but had the support of a strong linen interlining.

Underwear became important to both sexes. Many layers of linen were worn underneath the clothes and one prided oneself on a large trousseau, which must contain a sizeable number of chemises. Even if one still did not wash one's body, cleanliness was practised indirectly through frequent changes of the chemise. These layers also protected against the cold in the still badly heated houses. The more the heat the fewer, and the thinner, were the clothes, particularly underwear, that were necessary.

In those prudish times fashion did not lavish much thought on women's lingerie, except those parts which might on occasion become accidentally exposed such as the hem of the top petticoat which was embellished with beautiful English embroidery. Children and very young girls wore 'pantalettes' or 'mammeluks', drawers of lawn, which closed at the ankle with graceful ruffles, and were therefore just visible. The stage, musical revues, and operettas adopted the pantalettes as a symbol of Victorianism.

13 Crinolines and Hoopskirts

(1840–1867)

The economical and sober times of the post-Napoleonic wars were a thing of the past; the revival brought inventions,

74. A married couple in 1855. Satirical print by H. Daumier.

machines, factories, and traffic—steam locomotives, better carts, carriages, bicycles . . . Man was able to travel to the distant lands he dreamed of in earlier times, to the world expositions in Paris and London where all the miracles of art and science were on display. All this travelling produced a demand for more practical sportswear.

75. Crinolines of 1852 and of 1862.

The man

It was, of course, not necessary for men in factories and offices to wear corsets! Increasingly, they wore a colourless utility suit. The tailor, who in the previous period aimed to show through elegant cutting the swell of an arm or a leg, bent his efforts at making tube-like sleeves and pantlegs. The white shirt was barely visible under the black stock or cravat, the collar was lower, and no longer pricked chin or cheek. Only the military still wore corsets as support in riding, and broadened their shoulders. Subalterns and non-commissioned officers still had the 1865 rolls around the armhole; officers had epaulettes and already obtained some gauze stiffening in the shoulder region.

The woman

There were rumblings in the woman's world. To be sure, she still embroidered slippers, she still lisped 'yes', she moved slowly in the ever growing crinoline and sat down carefully, 'lest her feet became visible'. All opposition was suppressed until 1870 when it grew to a loud protest.

The sleeve's width descended in 1840, first towards the elbow and after 1850 to just above the wrist. In these wide, so-called 'Pagoda' sleeves, a bare underarm might be espied with some effort were it not that the young lady with demonstrative prudery filled the bottom opening of the pagoda sleeve with lace ruffles and widely ballooning undersleeves. The dress bodice was pulled tightly over the corset's smooth flowing shape. The bust made a single arch, real or imitation: the imitation was evidently widely applied as testimony to the advertisements in fashion magazines, which offered all sorts of paddings with fancy names that would shape the bust into a 'mono-bosom'. Secretive little pillows existed that filled the cleavage between the breasts and added some more

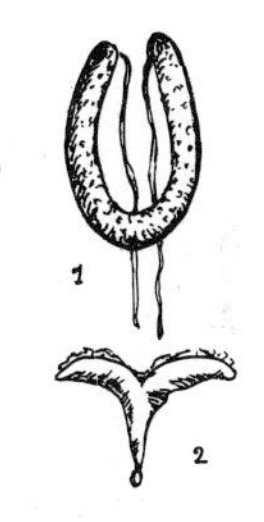

76. Two cushions for hip and breast padding. 1840, 1860. Costume Museum, Bath.

thickness at the top. The lacing of the waist was no longer such a problem; the skirts were so full that by comparison every waist appeared small.

Around 1840 women still wore a large number of petticoats, starched and quilted. Eventually the pelvis could no longer carry this weight! Women also worked bands of stiffened gauze into the hems of skirt and petticoat, but the circumference achieved never seemed large enough to them. These crinolines were about the same as those of the eighteenth century. Next came the hoopskirt, which could achieve much greater volume with much less weight. Over a simple petticoat and, sometimes, cotton drawers (either open drawers, split in the middle in order to enable, for example, the peasant in the field to urinate, or the closed variety, both with the pant-legs reaching below the knee) an ample skirt is now worn, which has steel hoops pulled through casings. Sometimes the hoops were removable, if the width of a carriage or a door did not allow enough room to accommodate the full circumference. The hoopskirt in fig. 78 is crocheted with a wide row of open-stitches at every turn through which the metal hoop, itself wound with yarn, could be braided. Half-hoops in the shape of a cheese cover, made out of sail-cloth and pulled over hoops of cane, also existed.

In such a cage the ravishingly beautiful Empress Elizabeth of Austria sailed through the Greek waters, visited Queen Victoria and her colonies; in the same way the equally ravishing Empress Eugenie of France, mounting mules and camels, travelled with her entire supply of Paris gowns over mountains to open the Suez Canal. The Dutch explorer Alexandrine Tinne traced the source of the Nile similarly attired. By means of an ingenious set of cords it was possible to pull up and shorten the skirts of the existing sports and travel clothes.

Shoes started to be made with small heels. At the same time it suddenly occurred to people that they had a right foot and a left foot. The use of the so-called 'curved last' could have provided relief for women's painful feet, but they were not enthusiastic about the idea. It had gradually become tradition that a shoe pinched and the lady (shoes were for her only, the common woman could not afford shoes) was barely

77. Hoops on red tape form a hoopskirt. Historical Museum, Göthenburg. c.1860.

78. Sports and travelling dress of lilac silk. E. Canter Cremers collection.

79. Inside of the travelling dress. In the middle front the joined strings can be reached through a split in the skirt, and with a single motion the skirt raised above the petticoat.

able to move anyway in those long skirts, trains, crinolines, and bustles.

The ladies of the second half of the nineteenth century were delicate creatures who did not exercise and became nervous from sitting at home. Their discomfort from walking in narrow shoes also strengthened the man in his conviction (or delusion?) that he was the strong protector of these helpless little persons.

It became more and more fashionable to be delicate and pale. The great success of the novel by A. Dumas-fils *La Dame aux Camélias*, a roman à clef concerning Marguerite Gautier, based on Marie Duplessis, who died of consumption, may have been one of the conspirators in starting this fatal fashion.

A young man did not have to put his girl friend on a swing, as in rococo times, in order to get a peek at her legs and underwear; the wide and lightweight hoopskirt floated like a cloud about her. On occasion it would tilt upward, even at such a tame game as croquet, and offer the careful observer a chance to satisfy his curiosity. The crinoline was a delightful subject for caricature and satirical prints: lovers and contraband could be smuggled under them and they could be used as parachutes and tents for camping! Near open fires these wide skirts of lightweight fabric (tulle, batiste, tarlatan) constituted a great danger. The worst disaster must have been the fire at the Maria feast in the cathedral in Santiago, where a tulle ruffle caught fire on a candle, and 2000 people perished as a result. In this manner Empress Elizabeth of Austria lost her sister the Duchess of Alençon in a burning ballroom in Paris.

It has been claimed that Empress Eugenie of France invented the hoopskirt when she was expecting her first child and wanted to camouflage her figure. That cannot have been the case. Already shortly after 1840 a start was made to lighten the load of the many petticoats with a single hoop; Eugenie did not marry Napoleon III until 1853.

Museum of Costume, Eridge Castle.
Muslin Dress and Shawl. Mid-1850's.

14 Bustles and Emancipation

(1867–1890)

The period of 1867–1890 was a time of many changes: man's social conscience was aroused. There were wars in and outside Europe; women's emancipation began; there were many innovations in technology, sports, and travel. The political map of Europe changed, most particularly with the rise of Germany and Italy to nationhood.

The man

Men who worked did not have much time to worry about their 'line'. Only the military uniform was made broad and sturdy in the shoulders, although without 'wings' and epaulettes. In men's clothing it became ever more difficult to show, or maintain class distinction. Only the white shirt, collar and cuffs still gave evidence that a man did not perform manual labour. In the case of festive evening wear—the tail suit—a lot of white shirt showed. The only means left to a man for showing his vanity was through his cravat (always visible around the neck), shirt-studs and cuff-links. The cuffs were now round, kept that way in round boxes (devotedly covered with embroidery); only in the twentieth century

80. Crinoline dress around 1855.

would the cuffs be pressed flat. Paper collars, coloured shirts, shirt-fronts, and half-shirts, were cheap and practical, but probably therefore little appreciated.

With the growing interest in sport the man rode a high bicycle, swam, played tennis, wrestled and took gymnastics at school. All this called for comfortably fitting clothing, which did not aim to impress, but would adapt itself to the demands of the sport in question. Supple warm underwear of basic design also came to be in demand for the same reasons.

The woman

Quite suddenly the crinoline became smaller in front, and at the sides; the fullness was moved towards the back, which was how the *cul de Paris*, or *queue de Paris*, or *tournure* came into being. But it was more than a mere change of fashion. Around 1870 the woman's role also changed radically. Many became students; societies were founded for the purpose of urging girls of good family to perform useful work. If a girl could not master anything except her embroidery needles, so be it, let her embroider, but let her sell the product, and so put an end to much silent poverty. Schools were founded where girls were trained to become teachers, bookkeepers, apothecaries ... The first nurses dared to enter hospitals among 'wardmaids' and 'wardservants'. All this found favour with the girls, who for a long time had had enough of sitting near the window, embroidering ('but turn down your eyes modestly, when a young man passes'). Now they had to stand proudly erect in order to show off a bustle to good advantage, which demanded a self-possessed bearing, and hollow loins. It was therefore not just a fact that the crinoline became more subdued in front and at the sides, it was also a different mentality that revealed itself. The new societies had been accused of catering for ladies only. Indeed, a woman of the working class needed no urging to work, night and day she already worked hard enough. At this time laws were widely passed which controlled and restricted the labour of women and children.

81. Silhouettes of 1873–1881–1887.

82. Queue: a cage of hoops over a crocheted petticoat. Historic Museum, Göthenburg. 1875.

Fashion now decreed trains; they fell most gracefully over a padding at the loin and seat-region. Even today the trains of bridal gowns receive a slight padding for that reason. The train was worn by rich and by poor, regardless of the difference in rank or welfare. But how could a charwoman do her work with a tail that swept the floor as ardently as her broom? A provision was made for this exigency: in the back, halfway down the thigh, her apron had a horizontal band, over which the train was pulled, consequently hanging behind her like a bag. After she had finished mopping the stairs, she would pull the bag down, and it was a train once more. A *queue* was a short crinoline cut in half, made out of bands of steel or whalebone, never reaching beyond the side-seams at the hip, and mounted on a lining. The bands, connected at the inside by tapes or elastic, could be tightened, thereby increasing the curve of the bustle and hence giving the gown a more sharply protruding silhouette. In addition, cushions were attached to the corset and the petticoat. This was topped by a petticoat with a train, which puffed over the cushions and had many ruffles of starched cotton or gauze.

83. Caricature of the tournure (bustle). Drawing by A. Grevin.

84. Corset of the pious Helena. Drawing of W. Busch.

Brassière, vile instrument of lust,
Shall nevermore support this bust!!

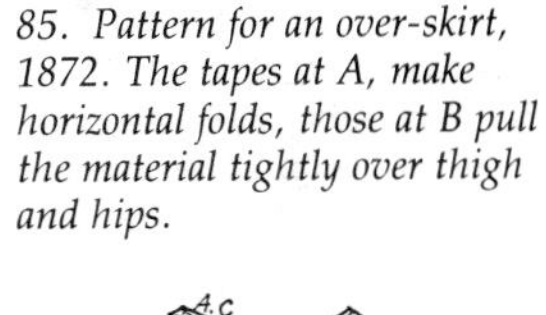

85. Pattern for an over-skirt, 1872. The tapes at A, make horizontal folds, those at B pull the material tightly over thigh and hips.

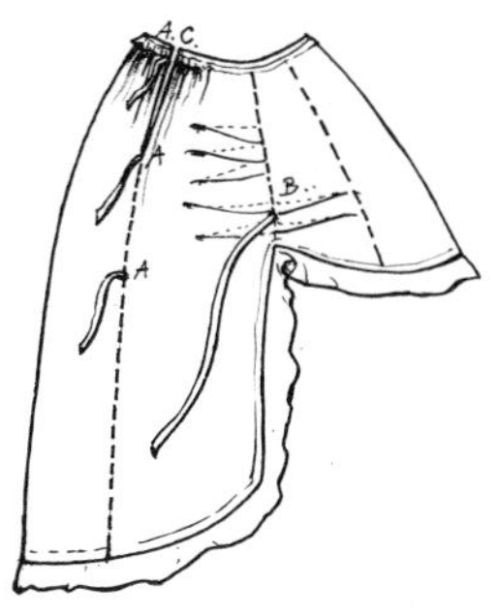

On top of all that went the gown, which had its own hip drapery.

How was it possible to sit with a bustle? The young girls in the upper classes of the 'École Française' (or another institution of learning), pushed it a little to one side and then 'the bustle was sitting next to you on the bench'. Very soon collapsible bustles were put on the market. Before anything else they had to be attached securely, because to lose it meant to be 'flat in the back'. No worse disaster could possibly occur.

86. Queue de Paris *of hoops in red wool. E. Canter Cremers Collection. c. 1885.*

While in English the word 'bustle' covers every back protrusion, there is a subtle difference between a *queue* and a *tournure. Tournure* is the nomenclature for the shape, the silhouette; the *queue de Paris* (Parisian tail) is the appliance which achieves that shape. The term *cul de Paris* (Parisian backside) was also used. Because at that time (between 1867 and 1890) a civilized usage of the language was appreciated, the word 'tail' was preferred over the name of the site where this appendage was attached.

In 1873 the Shah of Persia left his eastern palaces for the first time for a tour of the European courts. He saw to his amazement that all the princesses and court ladies had figures that were totally different from those of his slaves and harem women. Although, according to oriental mores, it is not proper to discuss women, he obtained information about this peculiar protrusion . . . 'these extraordinarily constructed skeletons, reinforced with hoops, which they called evening and ballgowns, must be ruinous to a woman's body, no matter how well it is shaped'.

The gowns were indeed excessively decorated, the lingerie was full of lace and flounces, the *décolletés* were cut low. All this may possibly have been a resistance against the emerging drive towards freedom, naturalness and simplicity.

The Shah wrote in his travel diary, 'At home no *sighe* (concubine) would dare to appear with such a *décolletage*, not even in the harem of her lord and master . . . Below the waist wives of the infidels pile layer upon layer of fabric and drape around thigh and legs the material of which the torso is deprived. Their bare arms and bosoms, covered only here and there by jewellery, in addition to an unveiled face, are in

87. Inside of the garment of fig. 86; by tightening the tapes the hoops curve more strongly outward.

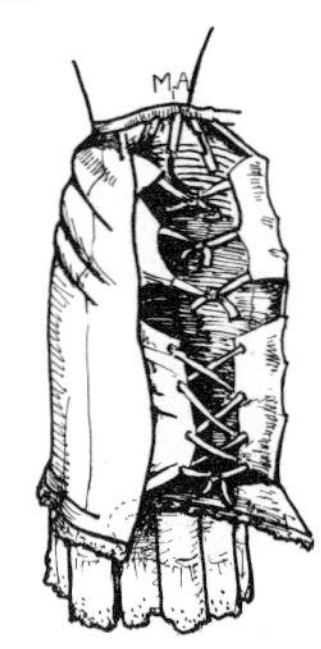

constant struggle with a strangling tidal wave of silk, velvet or lace in which the rest of the body suffocates . . .' Zola describes this time, and the fashion, as well as the great influence of the Parisian demi-monde, in his novel *Nana*.

Towards 1880, when women had had their fill of carrying this load of padding, folds and flounces and wished for a more slender 'line', it happened that a lady was shopping in a large emporium for corsets and lingerie. The head-salesman, who was in the back, called to her across the entire store, 'As I told you Madam, if you are a size three bust, you cannot wear a size four in hips.' This only goes to show that the stiff hour-glass silhouette of that time was not the natural 'line', even if the bustle was temporarily reduced in size. This hour-glass effect was notably reinforced by the sleeves, which were narrow at the upper arm, with high shoulders.

Dresses were buttoned tightly over corsets, breast and hips so that there was hardly any room for the fullness of the underclothes: these were now made of thinner fabrics, sewn tightly into shape, or made of a thin wool-tricot. In sports, which constantly gained in popularity, all this underwear was also a hindrance to both sexes. Sports, particularly tennis, archery, bicycling and sailing, promoted simpler and more friendly intercourse between boys and girls, and was a wholesome kind of marriage market.

Very soon the *queue de Paris* returned, but was very different in shape: more definite, almost square, protruding sharply. It happens at times that a fashion, which one fancies as a thing of the past, returns after a short time; then one eagerly embraces the old familiar silhouette, exaggerates it, until this 'line' disappears again, this time for good, or at least for a good long time. In fashion, of course, nothing disappears for good and nothing can be definitely of the past. Fashion is a constant struggle between conservative man who wants to preserve the old, and progressive youth who seeks the new, and *new* often happens to be the reappearance of that which has been forgotten.

Dresses were slimmer now, had no train, and much less trimming. The silhouette was pithy, smart, had a bright character and looked forward to an approaching new era for the woman and for society.

88. Wedding gown of cream wool E. Canter Cremers Collection. 1888.

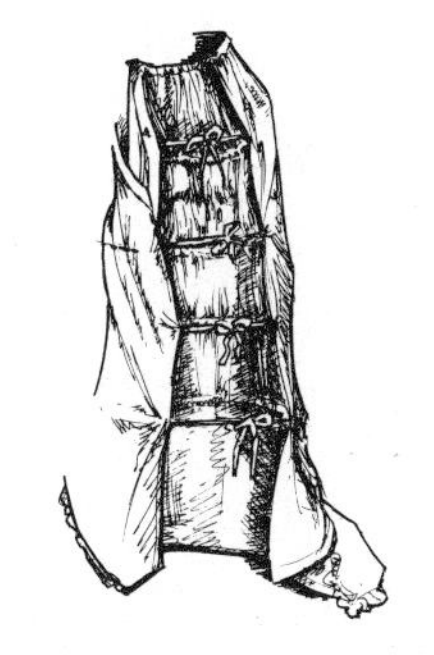

89. Inside of the wedding gown with four hoops. At the top a solid cushion.

90. Only a cushion raises the train of this dress. Hermitage, Leningrad, 1889.

A village laundress may have come across a combination-undergarment in the laundry of a progressive lady at this time. How was she to enter this strange article of clothing on the laundry list? She vaguely understood how the wind of fashion was blowing, and listed it as 'vegetarian drawers'. It is indeed the Vegetarian Movement that contributed much to what we now call 'leisure clothes'. The loose clothes, the sandals and the bare heads have remained. A woman's honour was no longer compromised if she wore flesh coloured hose, very thin ones, or none at all.

(1890–1914)

The erotic posture was never so fashionable as at this time and it was achieved in the following ways:
a) Through tight lacing and padding of the body until an entity of voluptuous curves had been created; b) Through allusion to lingerie; c) Through veiling and shrouding in a consummately subtle manner every part of the body, which would alternately be hidden and then revealed; d) Through a fashion which contributed to a pretence of frail health and thereby placed the man in the flattering role of the brave and strong protector of these delicate creatures.

a) When one says to an old gentleman: 'Your wife must have been very beautiful when she was young?' he will answer: 'Ah, yes, she had such a tiny waist!' He will show how he could span that waist with his hands, and he preserves the dog-collar, which she wore as a belt during their engagement. And yet these wasp-waisted creatures lived to a ripe old age and bore healthy children. Because the maid did all the work (except washing the breakfast dishes), they moved around very little, however, and ate food that was too calorie-rich and too vitamin-poor.

91. A small waist. Drawing by A. Guillaume, 1894.

The sensuous curves could be bought and many girls and women attempted to augment them further through the use of seductively advertised *pilules orientales*.

92. The foot in a black stocking becomes visible. Drawing by A. Guillaume, 1894.

b) Lingerie was not visible, it was only to be imagined. It may have been audible though, especially when two petticoats were worn of taffeta against moiré-silk under a simple woollen skirt. Then it took only a slight motion of thigh and hip to produce a soft rustle, the so-called 'frou-frou'. The train could be held up in a manner that revealed the hint of a pointed toe in a framework of lace, and ruffles. And it might just be revealed that, like the Parisian can-can dancers, she wore all-black hose. Solid, sensible women existed who ordered their underwear from the catalogue of a solid sensible store, and who knew how to tie their substantial husbands to them throughout their marriage, without silk, lace-trimmed drawers, without frou-frou whispering petticoats. But there were also those who in the bedroom enchanted their lord and masters with the magic witchery of an avalanche of sultry luxury: coloured lingerie, with silk ribbons laced through eyelet embroidery, the so-called 'laize frou-frou'; drawers which were now closed with a flap in the back, and had pretty ruffles at the knee; even nightgowns got ruffles at the wrist and in the middle front, and were tied with satin ribbons. A woman was no longer afraid to look seductive in her sleeping quarters, now that methods for birth control improved steadily.

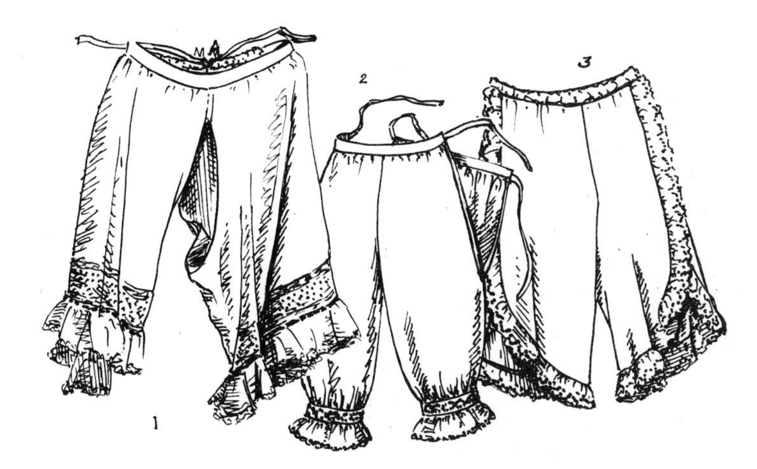

93. 1. Open drawers with lace, embroidery and laced-through blue ribbon. Worn in Indonesia c.1880.
2. Drawers with flap closing.
3. Closed drawers. French model. E. Canter Cremers Collection.

c) Veils were worn covering and attached to hats, which were trimmed with feathers and artificial flowers. These were more flattering and wrinkle concealing than the most expensive skin cream; crapy necks and double chins took refuge behind net collars, the 'guimps'. They were held erect by flexible bones, which pricked cheek and jaw. The lower arm was covered with lace fabric as, after 1910, half-sleeves were being worn. Blouses, dresses, and even coats were made of lace, now machine-made, with applications of Irish (crocheted) lace on net. At balls girls peeked over lace fans, and their chaperones wore lace bows against the chin, over their collars. On top of all this finery, now that houses were more adequately heated, shoulder capes of velvet and fur were worn, which enticed pawing and caressing.

94. Child from the Franz Sauer catalogue, c.1895.

d) Fainting, a powertool in the hands of a clever woman, to be used if she did not immediately get her way, was blamed on the tight corset. The real culprit in this drama was actually the tight collar, which obstructed the flow of blood to the brain. This fainting, the so-called 'vapours', and the headache, the 'migraine', may have given a lady more power than voting rights and legal equality.

Shoes were narrow and pointed, the heels uncomfortable. To be able to walk, a strong and gallantly offered arm was needed. The skin was pale, and the sun was kept out through

95. Leg o' mutton sleeves as contrast to the very small waist. Drawing by A. Guillaume, 1894.

under and over-curtains, as well as plush draperies. Outdoors, parasols, hats and veils offered protection against the sun. Around 1895 a 'line' develops which has a strong resemblance to that of the 1830s: a small waist, a wide skirt, broad shoulders and leg o' mutton sleeves that are kept bulging by all sort of artificial means, such as padding and support balloons. Even the apron of the young lady painting in fig. 95 helps to reinforce this line.

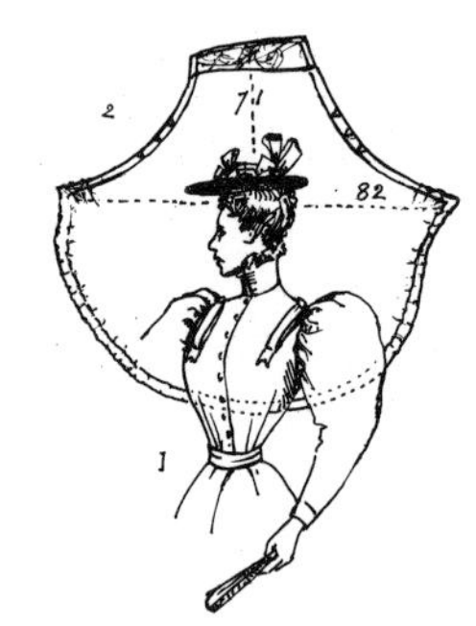

96. Pattern of the leg o' mutton sleeve. 1895.

Clothes expressed a difference of mentality and even of political convictions: the man oriented towards the left wore a low collar and a wide black bow-tie; his rightwing opposites plagued themselves with a stiff, high collar, up to 8 cm, a narrow butterfly tie, hair plastered down with pomade and parted from forehead to neck in what the Germans used to call 'ein Poposcheitel', and a carefully cultivated little moustache. Countless moustache-binders were recommended, which during the night pressed the moustache into the desired shape.

In women's clothing these differences were also visible: thick woollen chemises were worn by the spouses of socialists, girl students and working women but certainly not by the girl friends of Toulouse Lautrec and the many fun-loving princes, nor Sarah Bernhardt, the ravishingly beautiful gypsy Otera, Mata Hari, Yvette Gilbert, or Cléo de Merode. Although it did not behove man to criticize the works of the Creator, he always resented the fact that He put breasts on a woman's body. A monobosom might be tolerable, but two breasts were considered positively indecent. Therefore seamstresses made little pillows which, sewn inside the dress, would fill the cleavage between the breasts. Hence the corset industry constructed a single arch of fabric stretched over bones which reached from armpit to armpit. The reform movement did not get involved in this ticklish question and kept silent. The parents of children who had outgrown the fairy tale of the stork kept silent also. But two little boys looked for an answer to the question: one or two? the answer might be supplied by aunt Dolly. She had a voluptuous figure and on festive occasions a daring *décolleté*. The difficulty was that one thing or another had to be observed from above. It was Christmas and the entire family was gathered around the Christmas tree. Aunt Dolly was more voluptuous than ever, at least as seen from below. And then . . . on a chair on top of the buffet, a pious look at the tree-top's Christmas angel, a stealthy peek at auntie's bosom . . . and they knew! The family looked adoringly at the little one's fascination with that Christmas angel: so sweet, so innocent . . .

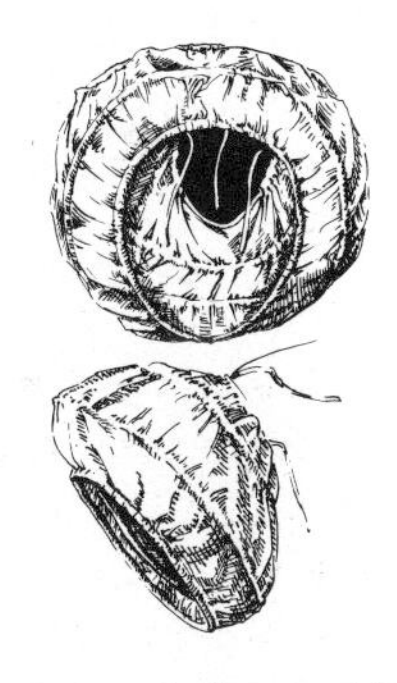

97. Support balloons, which were attached with tapes to the shoulders of the chemise.

The droit devant

This peculiar stance was obtained by pulling the back-muscles together in the loin region. The pelvis tipped forward, involuntarily. The foot turned outward, which resulted in walking with coquettish little tripping steps, and the hips moved along with every step. The shoulders were set low, the bust forward. This stance was certainly not uncomfortable and not unhealthy either. The physicians

98. Two ladies with the 'droit devant' figure (straight front, ergo, no stomach). English fashion plate, 1903.

were satisfied: the corsets which were worn lower no longer pressed the last rib inward and gave good support to the abdominal muscles. Elastic suspenders held up the stockings while holding down the corset, liberating the circulation from the necessity of garters around the leg, above or below the knee.

Many older ladies retained this body stance for the rest of their lives. Adorned still with lots of lace and flounces, ruchings and trimmings, this fashion can be called a farewell to the nineteenth century. A new 'line' would develop in 1908.

Children had had for some time a strange silhouette: a bulge in front. Boys had it above the midriff, girls below it. The girls carried a cotton bag on a string, like Lucy Locket:

Lucy Locket lost her pocket
Kitty Fisher found it.
There was not a penny in it
But a string around it.

Most often something would be in it: marbles, apples, slate-pencils, jacks. For the boys it depended whether or not there was a sturdy string in the bottom of the sailor blouses—if so, everything that was precious could be stuffed in it: dead mice, dirty handkerchiefs, slates and erasers; under this blousy garment one could even smuggle one's pet rabbit into school.

The 'Reform Movement' 1890–1914

Fierce, enthusiastic, and a bit aggressive, the emancipated woman was enthusiastic about reform clothing. Everything had to be 'logical' and 'honest'—there were to be buttons that did not serve as closings (those used for decoration only were not logical). There were to be no hidden snaps, for that was not honest, as then a bit of embroidery had to be placed over the snap, on that spot. In heaven's name no shape, no waist-

99. 1890–1914; Reform, the leg o' mutton sleeve and the small waist of 1894, droit devant 1904, the slender line of Poiret, 1911.

line, women had to be as straight as ramrods! In that way the 'Reform Movement' established its own taboos. A very illogical thing remained, however: the train, which swept up the dirt in the street and carried it inside the house. Another illogical item was the high collar which was also retained: if these were too tight they restrained the flow of blood to the brain, and could cause fainting spells.

Already in 1851 a new woman's costume had been introduced in America under the enthusiastic leadership of Mrs Amelia Bloomer. The storm soon passed into a mild breeze in USA and England. In Holland societies were founded, the so-called '5 Vs' (Vereeniging Voor Verbetering Van Vrouwenkleeding = Society for the improvement of women's clothing). Schools were started for women's labour, which trained reform seamstresses. Fashion and pattern-books appeared for that purpose. Gradually Scandinavia and Germany followed suit.

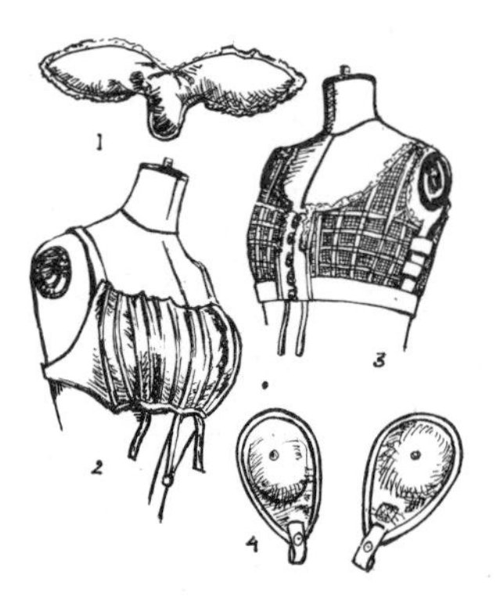

100. Brassières and additions: 1, 2, 4 fashionable. 3, Reform bra.

Later generations have mocked these reform clothes unjustly: the 'Reform Movement' established the relationship between clothes and hygiene, understood that the skin must breathe, that underwear had to be porous, liberated women from pinching bands around the waist which could damage the liver, and provided children and infants with comfortable, wholesome clothes.

The fight, however, was primarily against the corset. It was blamed for every disease from sore throats to corns. Doctors soon realized that a sudden omission of this support to weakened muscles was a danger. They said: 'A good corset is best, a bad corset is bad, no corset is worst.' The reform ladies fought on, even insisting on a legal interdiction against the wearing of corsets! It was to no avail and the battle of the corset was lost. Very soon the reform crusaders themselves started making 'reform-corsets, reform-bodices, and health-corsets'.

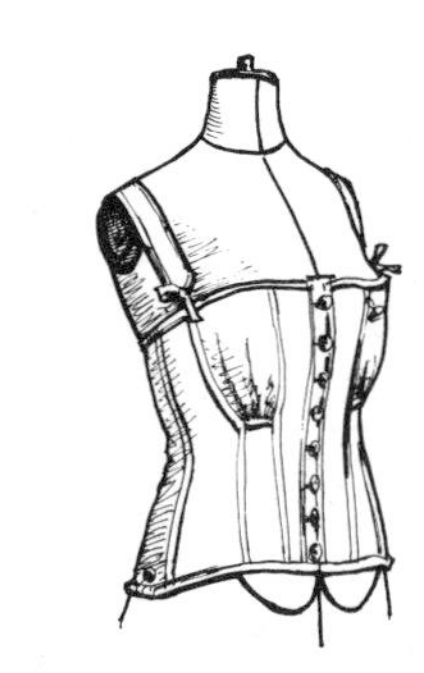

101. Reform corset bodice.

One might wonder whether there was a similar movement for men at the beginning of the century. And indeed there was, although for men there was not so much need for improvement since the battle of the corset did not involve them.

In Holland, for instance, on a fine summer day a pale

young man in Amsterdam might be seen walking dressed in a reform suit designed for him by H. Katzenberger of Munich. At his side was a young lady in a blue reform gown, and in a stroller behind the couple a baby wrapped in colourful blankets. They were followed by a few truant street urchins, but otherwise no one paid them any heed. Children's curiosity is easily aroused, but the ever sensation-hungry Amsterdamer prefers to look at an accident or watch a tough street fight than gawp at a suit of unusual cut. (Dr Jaeger also designed a reform suit with similar lack of success.) The above mentioned reform-family hailed from the Gooi region, a nature enclave south-east of Amsterdam, where followers of Tolstoy lived together in an idealistic commune, inundated with naturalists, theosophists, teetotallers, followers of the homeopathic methods of Pastor Kneipp, as well as anarchists and socialists. The vegetarians walked around in their sandals, bare legged and bare headed. A cape also belonged to this get-up.

102. Reform dress. Design P. Schultze. Naumburg, 1901.

The 'Reform Movement' made two mistakes:
a) It excluded the clothing profession. Furniture makers, sea captains, applied-artists, and vegetarians designed clothes that were impossible to make. The Paris haute couture, on the other hand, created for the working woman and student the (navy blue) tailor-made with the washable blouse, and also the 'trotteur', a sports-like pleated skirt, which was so audaciously short as to show the wearer's entire foot.
b) It forgot that man does not dress exclusively in order to be comfortably warm, and decently covered; it forgot that vanity and eroticism are the basis of fashion. The reform ladies were in favour of voting rights, and against eroticism; the woman must not be a man's 'lust-object'. That many young girls wanted very much to be some nice gentleman's lust-object no one dared to mention out loud.

One of the fiercest reform champions addressed a physician, listed all the detriments of fashionable clothing and the threats it posed to health, and said, 'Must we wear that stuff? Must we become ill?' The doctor reflected a while and finally said, 'Yes, go on and wear it—better a sick woman than an ugly one.'

103. Satirical print on the Reform fashion, 1904.

Poiret

The influence of one fashion designer should, by and large, not be over-estimated. Much of what is designed reaches the spring or fall fashion shows in Paris, Rome or Milan, but does not satisfy the infallible taste of the host of international buyers. No fashion will be accepted if the time is not ripe for it. A new fashion stimulates, until one is sated with its stimulation.

The man of 1908 had seen enough wiggling hips, bosoms and wasp-waists. It was no longer necessary to emphasize class distinction so strongly, times became more democratic, and the sports promoted fraternization.

Immediately upon returning from his shows in St Petersburg, Poiret sold his Russian notes. Many others did not and lost heavily in the money market. Through ever increasing swimming and bathing one became used to seeing the body's natural 'line', and in a time of increasing mobility such as motoring and bicycling a woman no longer had to be a stuffed corset, surrounded by far too many clothes.

In 1906 Poiret started his own fashion establishment. To his previous employers Doucet, and later Worth, he had been too revolutionary, too much influenced by modern painters and Russian ballets; here in his own house he could go his own way. He sensed what the women of that time needed and gave them slim, supple, simple clothes, made of soft fabrics over a few tricot underclothes (such as the 'directoire' drawers). The 'line' was long and slender, there was no corset; at the most, something sturdy to support the abdominal muscles and the bust. But because the women still demanded something that was uncomfortable, something that would impede their movements, skirts became so narrow that it was impossible to walk quickly, the more so because the enormously large hats had to be kept in balance atop the coiffure. They conquered this handicap with apparent grace and ease. In 1914 the skirts became wider and somewhat shorter. Women were now ready for the tasks the First World War would impose on them.

16 The Slender 'Line'

(1914–1930)

It was some years after the First World War before conditions gradually returned to normal and people no longer wore left-over trench clothes such as trench-coat rainwear. (It had been the fashion to work like the English officers in sporty tailor-mades, with a riding crop held under the left arm.) When it was no longer necessary to wear loose dresses to hide the results of a poor wartime diet, what is now called 'unisex' emerged.

At the time it was said, 'You simply cannot tell whether it is a man or a woman.' Jokes circulated such as, 'Give mummy and daddy a goodnight kiss.' The child answered, 'But I don't know which is mummy and which is daddy.'

Women's coats were cut in men's style, and shirts, ties, and felt hats were worn. Even more important was a very short head of hair: the 'Eton crop' was featured. Women wanted to resemble an Eton boy, thin and lithe and above all without a bust! The tight corsets flattened to some extent but some women resorted to surgery. The overwhelming success of the novel *La Garconne* will not have been alien to this 'line'. Also the loss of men through the war necessarily gave rise to much

104. Coat and skirt and enormous hat, 1908.

105. 1916–1920–1926. In 1916 the first short skirt, a scandal!

homo-eroticism: the strong masculine trend in women's clothes met this half way.

How was this beauty ideal, this boyish figure, achieved? Through dieting: eating as little as possible, swallowing lav-

106. A corset of 1904 and one of 1928.

ishly marketed diet pills, and breakfasting on a single lemon. The girls' mothers grew desperate, physicians shook their heads. But there were other difficulties! Ever since the Middle Ages it was the church which opposed every new fashion and banished it in vain. First it was the short hair of the female congregation that inspired priests and pastors to angry sermons: the cutting of hair was supposed to be *unnatural*. According to the ladies a clean-shaven preacher in the pulpit was just as unnatural. The result of all this preaching was that the so-called 'Dutch cut' of 1918 grew shorter still until in about 1924, with the Eton crop, the limit of cutting had been reached. And now the short skirts arrived! The transition from the time (around 1908) when the novel about Louise was considered pornography (she showed not only her feet but even her *ankles*) towards the barely covered boy's figure of 1925 was a very large one. For the churches this was understandably hard to digest.

107. The Eton-cut 1926: a moustache, how can I imitate that?

In many meetings of church councils the Protestant churches discussed at length whether or not to permit girls with short hair to the confirmation classes, and the meaning of I Corinthians II:5–6. The reaction of the Catholic churches was more positive. In the church portals clearly-stated directives were hung, regarding the permitted skirt lengths. That length crept upwards in a short time from foot to knee. Although in the fifteenth century the monk Thomas Connette was burned alive after his battle against large hats, which deprived the pious of a view of the altar, and although not a single interdiction of a new fashion had ever the slightest result Dutch Bishops jumped courageously into the fray. These gentlemen expected, according to their pastoral writing of March 1926, that the faithful should be covered from head to toe, only the hands and the feet being allowed to protrude beyond the clothing.

108. Unisex 1925. 'Excuse me Miss, I thought you were one of the boys.'

The bishops advised women and girls to join the 'Society of Honour and Virtue'. This organization published in 1926 a booklet 'Fashion Chats' written by an anonymous priest. It is a gruesome little book containing all the distressing things that can befall a follower of the fashions. He described in detail the death-bed of a certain Germana Duverseau, 'the victim of an immoral fashion'. She died in 1921 when 'short

109. *... And yet, short skirt and short hair! Drawing for 'the Catholic woman' by Jeanet Molkenboer, 1928.*

skirts' were not very short compared to the mini-skirt. The priest also cited the opening speech of the yearly general-meeting of Dutch Roman Catholic physicians on November 14 and 15, 1925. The speaker listed nine dread diseases which, according to him, would be contracted by women who wore short dresses and transparent blouses. Through the ages, fashion has indeed claimed many a victim; man happens to be a very imitative creature and it can be very difficult for a hedonistic woman to choose between *beauty* and *health*. The priest recommends his mother's gown: a stately garment of black velvet, 'beaded with thousands of jets ...'. It was of course inconceivable attire for women who smoked, danced the Charleston and worked in offices and factories. Were the factory workers supposed to go to their jobs in black silk and velvet and who could afford all those jets? The priest meant well, but how disappointed he must have been when, as soon as October 1928, the weekly paper *The Catholic Woman* accepted a fashion print which showed five ladies whose skirts were as short as their hair. Children wore long stockings, of course.

The solution to this indeed dangerous situation did not come about as a result of the good priest's fervent prayers; it came from a very different direction. What priests, anxious mothers, and angry doctors could not accomplish was achieved by a star in the movie firmament: Mae West. To the accompaniment of sensuous cooings she demonstrated that 'curves' and 'roundness' could have their charms all the same

110. *Mae West, 1934.*

and could stimulate the opposite sex which is, after all, fashion's primary goal. It worked: girls went back to eating breakfast, the symptoms of malnutrition disappeared. Grateful physicians bestowed an honorary degree upon Mae West: She had done more for the health of the American woman than the whole of medical science.

Although jokes about the body's 'line' in a period of fashion history are often revealing, the sailors' comments about Mae West's and her voluptuous shape must be considered unsuitable for this serious cultural study!

17 Cosmetic Surgery

In our time cosmetic surgery becomes an aid in achieving a desired 'line'.

In 1884 local anaesthetic was invented so it was no longer such an undertaking to have a wrinkle or a fat bulge removed. An operation for the latter had already been recorded three centuries earlier in the paintings of Jan Steen and Adrian Brouwer. From the painting one has the impression that it was no joke for the victim; for the observer it may have been considered some kind of country fair entertainment, just as footcare was.

It is claimed that around 1895 very vain ladies had their two lower ribs amputated in order to obtain a small waist. It is possible but unlikely. There was too much risk involved in such an operation, and ether or chloroform anaesthetics were very unpleasant. In any case, these two ribs are 'floating' and can easily be pushed in by the corset. Tight lacing offered another hazard if carried to extremes; the corset and especially the tapes could, if pulled too tight, make a deep ridge, which might ultimately damage the liver. Hence the propaganda, made by the 'Reform Movement', in favour of closings with buttons and button-holes. The corset pushed the liver partly upward, partly downward: upward it pressed into the lungs, impeding breathing: downwards it pressed into the abdomen making breathing practically impossible, which occasioned the much sought after 'heaving bosom'. To all the mysteries with which the 'fin de siècle' woman liked to surround herself this charming puzzle was now added: 'does she heave with emotion because a gallant gentleman whispers sweet nothings in her ear, or because she laced her corset too tightly?'

111. A normal liver in the normal place in the chest cavity, and another one, pushed away and deformed by tight lacing.

In America a clinic was opened with much fanfare and publicity in 1903 by Dr C. C. Miller, aged 22, which attracted hundreds of patients in search of youth and beauty. Was he a charlatan, a pioneer, or the clever inventor of ever new methods of surgery? His patients were considered guinea-pigs for his extraordinary methods, which he described in more than 40 books although he never published any photographs of before-and-after surgery. After him, older and more cautious doctors worked in this branch of surgery, which arose simultaneously in Europe. There was a great demand for face lifting, which involves the tightening and shortening of facial skin, so that wrinkles become less distinct. Plastic surgeons were able to do their most important work after 1918 and after 1945, when many succeeded in restoring the hands and particularly the faces of wounded soldiers to such an extent that the servicemen could reoccupy their place in society.

From about 1920 till 1930 there was another category of people who made demands on the services of plastic surgeons: the women who did not succeed in losing weight through a hunger-diet at the time of the 'slender line', and who begged the physicians to remove excess fat. Big hips might pass in a smooth, tight chemise dress, but a heavy bust was impossible. Did these women succeed in getting what they wanted? Cosmetic surgery had been considered a 'concession to sinful vanity' and psychology had occupied itself yet little with the pain caused by real or imagined bodily defects. We read in *Kort Amerikaans*, a novel by the well known Dutch author Jan Wolkers, how the leading character suffered because of a scar on his forehead, made visible by the prevailing short hairstyle. The question is: had the father permitted his son to cover his forehead with hair, would that have cured his neurosis or would he have been a nervous wreck for another reason?

Life and fashions change even faster:
Before 1930 we had to be as skinny as a rake, and less than 20 years later there was, for those with a nervous constitution, another reason to develop a complex: the American 'bosom culture' arrived on the scene and every woman considered herself flat-chested. There were plenty of gadgets on the market: from foam rubber hips, and stiff gauze sewn into dresses and petticoats, to pre-shaped bra's with 'cups' in all sizes. Even inflatable brassières could be kept up to par while dancing by means of a small tube, cleverly concealed in the *décolleté*. An American film showed workmen groping through piles of rubber breasts, and a doctor who pumped the contents of a large jar of yellow salve (paraffine or silicone?) into his patients' breasts.

There are women for whom the desire for a specific fashion 'line' is no 'sinful vanity' but a bitter necessity, in order to correct defects of nature and in so doing save her career and maybe her marriage. For her a soft place can be implanted which leaves barely a scar.

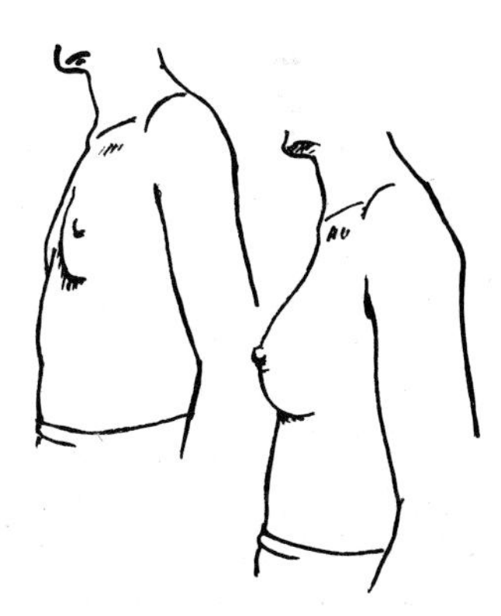

112. A Japanese woman is naturally flat chested, suited to kimono wearing. The second figure is able to wear Western clothes because of plastic surgery.

For Japanese women, a peculiar difficulty arose after the Second World War: by nature they are rather flat-chested, which the kimono style allows for, but after 1945 they sent American films parading gorgeous actresses with voluminous bosoms. They had started to wear western clothes made for western figures and they too desired that 'line'. There grew up in Japan a number of cosmetic surgery clinics, where tissues were implanted and where the Japanese man, who seemed to be very sensitive about his looks, submitted to operations on his eyes, nose and ears.

The romance had gone out of having one's ears pierced; it was no longer any fun. The surgeon did it quickly and efficiently, using a local anaesthetic. The goldsmith used a sterile tool for the same purpose. In the past there were old gentlemen who 'could do it so well' and who afterwards consoled the poor tortured souls for the pain they suffered.

18 The German Influence

(1930–1945)

All this unisex, those masculine suits for skinny, boyish figures with 'Eton-crops' . . . How did it all end?
a) A gradual lengthening of the skirts took place: at first, short in front and long in the back, with points at the side; after that it was long in the evening and calf-length during the day. Cutting fabric on the bias was a technical change, which made the clothes fall smoothly around the body, and in that way promoted the 'siren-line'. Underwear would make ugly folds underneath such skin-tight dresses; at most a tailored slip was worn in a tricot-like weave, or a 'chemise envelope' (chemise and drawers all in one) of pink *crêpe de Chine* with ecru lace. This was now sham-luxury, everything was machine made of cheap synthetic fibres, rayon, orlon, etc.

As a result of much swimming and sun bathing people became accustomed to seeing the human shape. Cushions and padding in order to produce a mono-bosom were the last things wanted. If any support was desired, there were 'step-ins' and 'grains' of elastic, rubber and lastex.

The Paris fashion houses kept on working, but after the financial crisis of 1929 it was hard going for them. Many went bankrupt: their clients could no longer afford the prices of these handsewn clothes. The rich and prominent ladies disappeared, the princesses were replaced by the queens of the silver screen. Schiaparelli dressed Mae West. American theatrical producers bought Paris originals and copied them for their revues. Later, Cardin made jackets for the Beatles. The marvellous gala-gowns of Worth were no longer suitable for the time: Poiret, never a businessman, retired after many disappointments to a village, where he painted until his death in 1944.

113. Puffed sleeves, ruchings and ruffles as in 'dirndls'. American 'Vogue', 1938.

114. Flowered fabrics and jabots from 'le Jardin des Modes', 1936.

b) Second only to Paris, Berlin was a fashion centre with a difference: Paris clothed the more mature, sophisticated woman, Berlin the wholesome young girl. The German fashion magazines added a column 'elegant-sportliches'. German fashion also had an aesthetic side to it, keeping contact with the applied arts and taking inspiration from the Bavarian and Austrian regional clothes. Suddenly one saw, even in the American edition of Vogue, dirndl type blouses with puffed sleeves, slanted Tyrolean hats with a feather, suits with grey-green forester's jackets. Young people of that time saw things they had never seen before, but which their grandmothers still remembered: hats with flowers and veils (many, flattering veils) and artificial flowers (the old Charleston dresses had at best one bouquet on the left shoulder, but that was all). There were white cuffs and collars with starched and fluted ruchings and ruffles. Who even remembered what starching and fluting was? Soft colours become blonde women, particularly sky-blue and sweetly flowered fabrics, which long survived the German influence and the war. Suddenly capelets were back again and muffs and gloves; it was like a nineties revival!

115. An English lady at a cricket match in 1935: lace, ribbon, long gloves, hat with flowers.

New in the 'line' of that era was an accentuation of the shoulders. The tailors of the ready-to-wear industry increasingly used gauze and padding in the shoulder region on clothes for both sexes. For the man this happened gradually, for the woman it was something new: these small shoulder pads give the silhouette a clean-cut trim look. For two reasons the German influence, so shortly before the Second World War, roused no political objections. In the first place, its impact on a specific period is discernible only many years later. Secondly, fashion transcends politics and wars. The Dutch took to wearing the Spanish ruffs during their Eighty Years' War against Spain, as well as adopting Empire gowns during the French occupation.

Since National Socialism contained a certain 'back-to-nature' element, the 'line' was a natural one, nothing was pushed away, nothing was padded, only the legs seem to be lengthened through the wearing of thick wooden or cork soles, but that was out of necessity. These ingredients do not lend themselves to the making of thin soles, and leather was impossible to get.

In the years before the Second World War all textiles were used for soldiers' uniforms. Out of the little that remained for civilian use, fabrics were made from all kinds of synthetic fibres, and for the woman there were all kinds of lace: it covered the skin and kept one warm, although more than half of it was nothing but air. Above all, it was not rationed! During the war it became a challenge to make something out of nothing: dresses out of tablecloths, coats out of woollen blankets, raincoats from water-proof sheets, blouses from dish towels, etc., etc. When even those articles were no longer available, one new item was made out of two old ones. Shoes were made out of a combination of cork, nail heads, skate-straps and oil-lamp wicks. The results of these home-crafts were often surprisingly attractive.

French fashion magazines featured seductive pictures of 'trench-wear': soft woollen dressing gowns which one could put on hastily in the case of an air-raid alarm. One would gladly surrender one's last ration coupons for that!

For a slender 'line' this was an advantageous time due to the wartime rationing of food.

116. War fashions: one new out of two old ones. 1940.

117. Bavarian influence. American 'Vogue', 1947.

19 After 1945

Man has the strange characteristic of craving exactly that which it is difficult to obtain. After the First World War when leather could not be bought for love or money, women wanted to cover that small part of their legs which became visible under their shortening skirts with high laced boots. After 1945, when bodies were barely covered as a result of years of textile rationing, followed by the bartering of the last remnants of one's clothes for some black-market beans, the 'New Look' arrived. Yards and yards of fabric from circular skirts suddenly swung around us. Dior had tried in vain to introduce that silhouette in 1938, but he succeeded the second time around. The 'line' remained normal: nothing was added, nothing was pared down. Something was added to the man's silhouette though. He wore much heavier shoulder padding. At the moment when the small pads women wore between 1934 and 1950 were on the way out, the man's back, chest and shoulders were made broader than ever before. This rigid shoulder-line has become somewhat more pliable only in our present time, with the much more nonchalant leisure-wear.

118. The New Look, model Maggy Rouff, 1948.

Soon after 1950 skirts became a little shorter (but, according to our present day notion of the word, still very long) and fashion also demanded that they be narrow, and waists small, to contrast with rounded hips and bosoms. Such demands no longer presented a problem. America supplied 'falsies' of sponge rubber or foam-plastics in all sizes and prices. Elegant 'waist-sinchers', old fashioned once more with lace and ribbon trim, or 'Merry Widows' of black satin with ruchings and long suspenders, did not serve any longer to lace-in the waist, but to attach rubber hips and buttocks. The compression of the ribs makes sense no longer, life is too fast for that, the fashions change more and more frequently, and we know that our 'line' will have to be changed again, before any reshaping has been achieved.

The American bosom culture leaves nothing to the imagination about the shape of the breasts: the many ways of obtaining this fashionable 'line' have already been detailed in chapter 17.

Women take more and more to wearing trousers: at first for sports, work and vacation, but in the 1960s the trouser-suit became day and evening-wear as well.

119. Beatle—dress. E. Canter Cremers Collection. 1964.

1960

And so the changes in fashion quietly flowed on—we talked about A, B, and H lines, about maxi, midi, and mini-skirts—until something happened that shook Europe to its foundations: the Beatles arrived. There were not enough police to protect them from the oppressive enthusiasm of their 'fans'. The conversation was not about their music, nor about the originality of their presentation, but everyone trembled and raved about their hairdos. It seems odd to reflect that 15 years ago their hair was considered *long*. And at least their hair was neatly combed and cut, while their jackets had been styled in Paris by Cardin.

After this all hell broke loose. It became fashionable for men and women to dress in an intentionally slovenly manner (which men had done before for example in the seventeenth century, and at the time of the French Revolution). This sloppy way of dressing, which was more marked than ever before may have been encouraged by the sale of American army-surplus clothes. Young men now wore battle-dress, parkas, fatigues, and a little later they all wore the loose 'Truman-shirts'. And let us not forget blue-jeans, preferably dirty, faded and frayed! It was not until 1970, however, that spots and patches were printed on machine-faded fabrics. This intentional sloppiness might be nothing new for young men, but it was so for girls, who had never before been observed wearing pants, sweaters, and clothes of all different kinds of fabrics sewn together as long as it was comfortable and sloppy. She even went as far as letting her hair grow long and hang loose. Was there no more female vanity? Of course there was, only it was directed to a carefully studied carelessness: towards extremely short skirts, hot pants, and T-shirts that constantly crept up, so that the bare midriff showed.

Since 1970 young people have distinguished themselves from the older generation by wearing long hair and eccentric clothes. In so doing they make the generation gap as wide as possible. The manufacturers cater for them, for they spend much of their salary on clothes, even if they do not save their money, or pay their parents room and board! Expensive clothes are no longer sold in the hours when 'ladies' go shopping, but hastily during lunch breaks from the office. The time when fashion served to indicate rank and social position is past: democracy no longer desires it, and futhermore the news media see to it that everyone knows when X or Y has reached a higher rung on the social ladder. They no longer need to demonstrate this through ample, costly garments, and plumed hats.

20 Up-to-Date

Hippy youngsters radiated love of humanity. With their long hair, beards, and frayed blue jeans they were as happy as children. They were politically aware and wanted to reform society. (Perhaps one can compare them with the 'Incroyables' and 'Merveilleuses' of the French Revolution.)

In the capitals of the world they sat on the steps of national monuments and at the international airports constituted the most important tourist attraction, without receiving any payment for it. Their fashions were created in London and New York, and influenced Paris. They looked as dirty as possible, but would gratefully accept the offer of a shower or a bath. Young people became increasingly environment-conscious and were therefore anti the use of chemicals for man-made fibres. Now, they want to wear real fabrics; there is much demand for real linen, and bobbin lace. Even make-up must contain something 'natural' in order to sell well: macrobiotic powder for the skin and lipstick with hormones sell like hot cakes.

Possibly as a reaction to so much steel, glass and concrete, a romantic yearning has emerged for the 'good old days', for grandpa's moustache, grandfather's chair, and granny dresses. This nostalgic mood produces long skirts, hats with flowers and veils, printed fabrics, puffed sleeves ... everything mentioned in chapter 18. The younger generation is also charmed by early twentieth-century objects and finds them desirable. They have a soft spot for the most ordinary articles from the beginning of the century, like mangles, oil lamps, washbowls, etc. (to the benefit of the antique trade).

What does the future hold? After the 'granny dresses', will the great-grandmother's corsets and wasp-waists make a comeback with all the migraines and vapours that went with them? And the cars? Will the fact that our young people have sat in small cars year after year change their shape? In addition to heart attacks, will car bellies and sagging hips be common in future? Perhaps not. Cars are no longer such status symbols. Many a young woman now holds two or three large dogs on a leash. Can we therefore expect gowns with a short left and a long right sleeve because of the arm which was stretched by those pulling dogs? Time will tell.

120. Trousers which make the legs appear longer, 1974.

1975

How was the 'line' in 1975? Still skinny. (Observe the variety of diet products and the popularity of slimming institutes. Josephine Baker, the singer, died suddenly in the spring of 1975. According to her friends, her untimely death cannot be attributed to the enormous strain of a 3½ hour performance on a 69 year old woman. It is suspected rather that the slimming pills the singer swallowed incessantly weakened her too much.)

A bosom was no longer a necessity neither was underwear. For a young man there was a pair of under-shorts, and if it was very cold a cotton T shirt. For the girls a body stocking or panty hose sufficed. A small head and long legs were desired by both sexes. Fashion photography with its distorted perspectives may have encouraged the latter. The surgeon could not yet give the head a different dimension; to lengthen legs might have been possible, but it was too serious an undertaking for the sake of fashion, which is intrinsically transitory. Instead thick soles and high heels were added to the shoes and boots of both girls and boys. The trousers were worn very low on the foot and rose very high at the waist. The distance from waist to foot suggested a very long leg. Sweaters became shorter. The head also *appeared* small: the boys wore a shorter coiffure, covering the forehead and part of the cheeks, which suggested a small face. Girls wore very curly half-long hair (the poodle-cut) also covering much of the forehead. Rouge carefully applied high and outwards on the cheekbone could also make the face look smaller.

Little was changed in the body's 'line'—nothing was 'added', nothing was 'pared down'. Models at fashion shows presented a slouching posture and bent knees. This may have been furthered by the current chairs or pillow-seats on which it was only possible to lounge languidly, and which were unsuitable for sitting erect at a work table.

The Present

Fashion may often be painful, but sometimes it is just the opposite. 'Jogging' is all the rage: a search for wholesome mobility to counteract the immobility forced on us by riding in cars. For jogging one dons the soft pliable track suit that vies in popularity with blue jeans.

The wearers of boots with heels so high that walking becomes almost impossible naturally do not participate in jogging. Let us hope that those boots are made of leather which is at least porous. Leather boots are expensive, however, so plastic ones will be worn, enclosing the lower leg tightly. The foot cannot 'breathe' in this, the skin suffers and becomes macerated, blistered or worse. But a young lady who has happily acquired such a pretty pair of boots just like her girlfriend's cannot be convinced of that. With boots above the knee, a waistlength jacket, and in-between a pair of light-coloured or white pants, which are getting tighter all the time, the shape of buttocks and lower belly are no longer the secret of either sex.

The hair which many men wore down to their shoulders is shorter now and 'permanently' waved into an 'Afro' hairdo. The sharp rise in popularity of the beard is a possible reaction to all the 'unisex' clothes. Here at least is something masculine, that women cannot imitate. But, despite unisex, men continue to close their garments left over right, thereby maintaining the role of the hunter or warrior, who has to reach for his sword with his right hand, before the enemy can overpower him, or the animal he hunts can devour him.

One puzzle remains: why do people in Moscow and in New York simultaneously insist on a specific pair of fashionable spectacle frames? Why do men in Norway and in Argentina get excited about a jacket with *narrow* lapels at the same time, and why are those jackets in demand again a few years later all over the world? (i.e. in those parts of the world where Western clothes are worn). Why do women in Mexico suddenly want skirts with pleats or godets, and why do those in Australia and Spain want exactly the same thing? Is it because the news media make rapid communications so easy? Indeed not. It has always been so. Around 1910 all the women in the Western world bent forward simultaneously and pulled their back muscles together in order to achieve the *droit devant* figure. This book offers no solution to this puzzle.